Illustrated by:

**Colin Andrew   Peter Archer   Shirley Bellwood
Brian Bysouth   Mike Cole   Andrew Howat   John Lobban
Peter Morgan   Ted Osmond   Pat Owen   Ron Rutterford**

Acknowledgements

The illustration on page 60 is reproduced by courtesy of His Grace the Duke of Portland and that on page 14 of Mr P. Maxwell Stuart of Traquair.

Photographs
ANP Foto, Amsterdam 153; Beardsley Theobalds, Nottingham 76–77; Bildarchiv Preussischer Kulturbesitz, Berlin 29 inset right, 78 bottom left; British Museum, London 127; Bundesarchiv, Koblenz 35 inset, 83 top right; Col. S. I. Derry, Newark, Nottinghamshire 118 inset top left; Crown Copyright – Department of the Environment 60–61; Mary Evans Picture Library, London 42–43; Hamlyn Group Picture Library 14–15, 112–113; Hamlyn Group Picture Library – John Freeman endpapers; Keystone Press Agency, London 118–119; Layland Ross Ltd., Nottingham 60 inset; Mansell Collection, London 90 top left, 103 top; Ministerie van Defensie, The Hague 51 inset top left; Musée Nationaux, Paris 128; Nordisk Pressefoto, Copenhagen 71 inset top right; Scottish National Portrait Gallery, Edinburgh 14; Spectrum Colour Library, London 144–145; Commander F. Steinmetz, Amstelveen 51 inset top right; Swiss Tourist Office, St Gallen 111; Z.E.F.A. – G Seider 107.

The photograph on page 106 is reproduced from A. J. Evans, *The Escaping Club*, the Bodley Head, London, 1921.

The Hamlyn Book of

Great Escapes

Brenda Ralph Lewis

Hamlyn
London · New York · Sydney · Toronto

First published 1978 by
The Hamlyn Publishing Group Limited
London · New York · Sydney · Toronto
Astronaut House, Feltham, Middlesex, England

ISBN 0 600 33161 X

Printed in Great Britain

Contents

Introduction

'Freedom' is one of the most inspiring words in any language. It takes many forms – physical, religious, social, intellectual, political, cultural – and there has never been a time in history when human beings have not been willing to bend all their energies towards the task of preserving all or any of these liberties. They have fought, suffered, killed and died for it. They have been willing to face the direst hazards simply for the sake of being free.

Only this compulsion can explain what all the escapers in this book have in common, and why all those who put themselves at risk to help them acted as they did. In ordinary circumstances, most were ordinary people, not especially brave or enterprising and certainly with no idea that confronting death and danger was exciting. But once caged, these ordinary people changed, and turned their minds, energies and ingenuity to one purpose only: escape.

Elios Toschi, for instance, escaped many times before he finally succeeded in eluding his captors. Heinrich Harrer climbed the Himalayan mountains. Franz von Werra jumped from a moving train and traversed a frozen river. Thomas Tibbles ran through a pitched battle with bullets whistling all around him. Graeme

Warrack sealed himself in a cramped hole beneath a roof as he waited for his chance to break out of prison camp.

Among the helpers, practically the whole population of Denmark deliberately risked the most brutal reprisals from their Nazi conquerors to spirit away almost all the country's 7,000 Jews across the water to Sweden and safety. In neighbouring Norway, the fjords of the west coast were regularly visited by Norwegian fishermen who crossed the North Sea in its most savage season to rescue fellow-countryfolk in danger, or land arms, ammunition and agents to help the resistance movement fighting Nazi tyranny. Graeme Warrack was sheltered by a Dutch family who knew that if things went wrong and they were caught, the men among them would be shot and the women and children sent to face the horrors and deprivations of a concentration camp. What is more, Warrack was only one among hundreds: while he got away, his hosts remained behind, in constant danger of discovery.

This book of escape is therefore not just a book of thrilling adventures, hair's-breadth risks, tense suspense or courageous deeds. It is also a record of the extraordinary lengths people will go to for the sake of freedom – their own or someone else's.

CHAPTER 1
Flight from the Tower

*Inside the cell, Lady Nithsdale
set to work to turn her husband into a
replica of Mrs. Mills.*

The snow and icy wind whipped hard at the Countess of Nithsdale's face as she spurred her horse to greater and greater speed along the snow-smothered road. Her companions, her maid Evans and a groom, had a hard job keeping up with her. Snow and ice sprayed up under the racing hooves, soaking the riders up to the waist and chilling them through and through. At any moment, all three riders knew, their mounts could stumble on a hidden hillock or a lump of snow, or might get a hoof caught in one of the innumerable small holes that peppered the road. To be thrown from the saddle at the speed they were going could well be fatal, but there was no slackening of the breakneck pace. Lady Nithsdale had one thought in her mind: to get to London as soon as possible, and every minute taken up by the journey was one minute nearer the execution of her husband, William Maxwell, Fifth Earl of Nithsdale.

If she could get to London in time, she might just be able to save him. If King George would heed her pleas, he might, even at this late hour, pardon Lord Nithsdale and free him from that dank, daunting place of terror and doom, the Tower of London.

In February 1716, Lord Nithsdale and four other Scottish lords were in the Tower awaiting death for their part in the Jacobite rebellion of the previous year. Fear often makes people, governments and kings included, act with great harshness and this had certainly been the case with the reaction of the English when, in 1715, Scottish Jacobites attempted to replace their new Hanoverian king, George I, with James Stuart of the Royal House of Stuart.

Once, the Stuarts had been kings and queens, not only of England but of Scotland as well. In fact, the first Stuart monarch, who came to the throne in 1603 was King James I of England and VI of Scotland. However, the English had never been completely happy with James or his son, King Charles I (1625–1649), or grandsons Charles II (1660–1685) and James II (1685–1688). For one thing, the Stuart monarchs were Catholics, if not in practice then in sympathy, and if there was one sort of ruler the fiercely Protestant English could not bear it was a Catholic ruler. Worse still, the Stuarts were far too fond of thinking of themselves as rulers appointed by and responsible only to God. 'The divine right of kings' this idea was called, and in practice, it meant that a king could rule by himself and did not have to consult or take advice from his nobles, or Parliament or anyone else. The English hated this idea. They were used to monarchs who ruled with the help of noble or parliamentary advisers and in the past, they had fought wars against kings who refused to comply.

In these circumstances, it may seem a miracle that any Stuart king or queen was ever able to stay on the throne of England. The ones who managed it were either clever and cunning like James I or Charles II, or they were known Protestants, like the joint rulers King William III and Queen Mary II (1689–1702) and their successor Queen Anne (1702–1714). It was a very different story with the other two Stuarts, Charles I and James II. The English Parliament quarrelled so violently with Charles over his belief in the divine right of kings that civil war broke out in 1642. Parliament won and put the

Lady Nithsdale spurring towards London in a desperate endeavour to save her husband's life

king on trial as a traitor; he was found guilty and was beheaded in January 1649.

After that, England – and Scotland – were ruled by Oliver Cromwell, Lord Protector, and by Parliament for eleven years. It was a dismal time, overshadowed by guilt over the murdered Charles and before long, the people began to long for a monarch again. In 1660, after Cromwell's death, there was great rejoicing throughout the country when the dead king's son, another Charles, returned to Britain from exile in Europe as Charles II. Charles II, like his father, had Catholic sympathies and believed in the divine right of kings. However,

11

unlike his father, Charles II was clever enough to keep his beliefs to himself. Better to do that, Charles II thought, than go into exile once again. Charles's subjects, and his Parliament, also had a special fear – a fear of another civil war – and because of this they were willing, though sometimes only grudgingly, to put up with Charles II's brother and successor, King James II.

With James II, who came to the throne in 1685, the English Parliament and people had to show a great deal of tolerance. James was the most unsuitable of all the Stuarts, even worse in some ways than his father, King Charles I. For one thing, the rather stupid and very stubborn James was a devout Catholic and as soon as he became king, he tried to turn England into a Catholic country, appointing Catholic ministers and openly practising his religion in spite of vigorous protests from his Protestant subjects. However, even then they were willing to swallow their anger and endure the dreadful James because his two daughters and successors, Mary and Anne were declared Protestants. Eventually, these two women would succeed James, England would become Protestant again and all would be well.

Then, in 1688, this prospect was completely overturned. In that year, James's second wife, also a Catholic, gave birth to a son, James Francis Edward Stuart. The English were appalled. This Catholic child, not Mary and Anne after all, would come to the throne after James II. There now stretched ahead an endless line of Catholic monarchs. It was too much. James II was deposed and exiled with his wife and son, and in 1689, the crown was offered jointly to Mary and her Dutch Protestant husband, William of Orange. They became King William III and Queen Mary II and were succeeded after William's death in 1702 by Mary's sister, Queen Anne.

James Francis Edward Stuart was then nearly 14 years old and he had spent all but a few months of his life as a dispossessed emigre. In 1701, the year his father died, the boy's hopes of retrieving the throne were dashed by the

Act of Settlement in which the successor to Queen Anne, should she die without heirs, was to be the Protestant Elector of Hanover. The Elector, George, was a great-grandson of the first Stuart monarch, King James I.

On Queen Anne's death in 1714, Elector George became King George I and with this, James Francis Edward and the supporters of the Stuarts in their native Scotland made a bid to retrieve the lost Stuart crown. The Earl of Nithsdale was among them. In September 1715, the Scottish Jacobites – 'Jacobus' was James in its Latin form – rose against the new king. The rebellion was, however, a speedy failure. The Stuart forces were thrashed in battle at Sherrifmuir and in November 1715 at Preston, where Lord Nithsdale was among several rebels captured.

Six of the rebels, including Nithsdale, were brought to London and taken through the streets of the city to the Tower. Preceded by drummers and trumpeters, the captives were forced to walk to prison with their arms bound behind their backs, like criminals. A jeering crowd lined the streets to watch.

The rebel lords being taken through the streets of London to captivity in the Tower

The ten-day trial of Lord Nithsdale and the other Jacobites ended on 19th February, 1716, when sentences of death were passed. When the terrible news that her husband was to die reached Lady Nithsdale at her home at Torreglas in Dumfriesshire, she determined at once that she must save him. Immediately, she had a horse saddled and set off for Newcastle. There, she hoped to take the mail coach south. But when she arrived at Newcastle, she found to her horror that heavy snowfalls had blocked the road and the mail coach might not be leaving for several days.

Lady Nithsdale painted by Sir John Medina

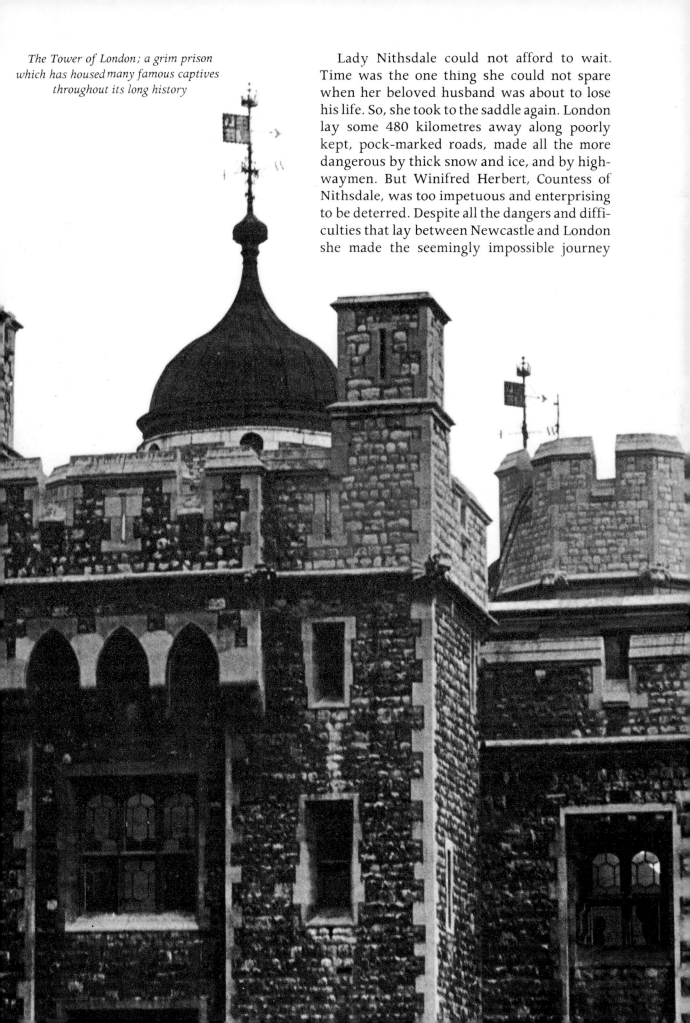

The Tower of London; a grim prison which has housed many famous captives throughout its long history

Lady Nithsdale could not afford to wait. Time was the one thing she could not spare when her beloved husband was about to lose his life. So, she took to the saddle again. London lay some 480 kilometres away along poorly kept, pock-marked roads, made all the more dangerous by thick snow and ice, and by highwaymen. But Winifred Herbert, Countess of Nithsdale, was too impetuous and enterprising to be deterred. Despite all the dangers and difficulties that lay between Newcastle and London she made the seemingly impossible journey south and at last arrived in the capital. She was travel-stained, exhausted and in a fever of anxiety but she learned, to her intense relief, that her husband was still alive.

Lady Nithsdale went straight to St. James's Palace where she pushed her way past servants and attendants and quite literally threw herself at the feet of the king, George I. She clutched at the hem of his coat, begging for her husband to be pardoned and although the king tried to shake her off, she refused to let go. When he attempted to escape from the room, Lady Nithsdale clung on doggedly and was dragged along on her knees by the bemused and infuriated monarch. Eventually, one of the king's attendants grasped Lady Nithsdale round the waist and held her, while another prised her fingers away. It was no easy task. Lady Niths-

dale was struggling frantically all the time to thrust into the king's pocket the mercy petition she had brought with her.

King George, doubtless relieved to be rid of an apparently hysterical madwoman, vanished from sight. Lady Nithsdale, according to her own account of the incident, 'almost fainted away from grief and disappointment' at her failure to obtain the pardon she had so ardently sought. There was only one other alternative: to plan her husband's escape.

Escape from the Tower of London was nothing new in 1716. Prisoners across the six centuries that the great fortress had stood by the River Thames had bribed their way out, shinned down the outside walls with the aid of ropes or sheets or had picked the locks of their cells. Some had managed to saw through the bars and, in fact, one of Lord Nithsdale's fellow rebels, Lord Winton, had cut his way out of the

Lady Nithsdale begging King George I for her husband's life. Petitions for mercy for serious crimes were not uncommon in the eighteenth century. Pardons could also be bought for a high price

Tower in precisely this manner and escaped across the Channel to France.

The most frequent method of escape, by rope, had already been used once too often by the time the Countess of Nithsdale was contemplating ways and means of freeing her husband. Special security precautions had been taken against any further repetitions of this method and more devious plans were therefore required. Lady Nithsdale's plan was a mixture of cunning, audacity, carefully stage-managed deception, charm – and luck.

The Earl of Nithsdale was one of three Jacobite lords due for execution on the morning of 24th February. Two days earlier, Lady Nithsdale went to the Tower. With her she took a headdress and some face paint, which she concealed in her husband's cell in the Queen's House. The next night, the night before the execution, Lady Nithsdale returned with three companions – her maid, Evans and her landlords in London, Mr. and Mrs. Mills.

While the first two waited outside, Lady Nithsdale took Mrs. Mills to the Earl's cell, where the landlady stripped off the extra dress she was wearing under her cloak. Lord Nithsdale put this on quickly, while Mrs. Mills went back down the stairs, ostensibly to fetch Evans. As she went, she made a great and very noticeable show of tearful distress, bewailing the impending fate of Lord Nithsdale and sobbing into a handkerchief held to her face.

Inside the cell, Lady Nithsdale hurriedly set to work to turn her husband into a replica of Mrs. Mills. She painted his thick, dark eyebrows so that they looked like Mrs. Mills's sandy coloured ones, placed the headdress on his head – it resembled Mrs. Mills's hair – and rubbed rouge onto his face and cheeks.

Mrs. Mills now returned to the cell, her face still buried in her handkerchief, took off her hood and replaced it with another which Lady Nithsdale had brought specially for her. The landlady then dried her 'tears', put away her

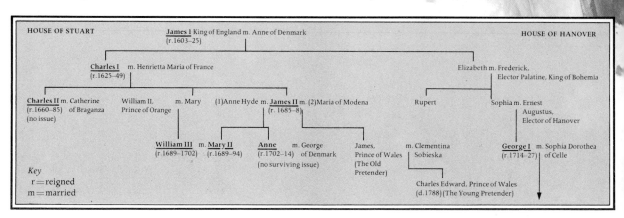

HOUSE OF STUART						HOUSE OF HANOVER
	James I King of England m. Anne of Denmark (r.1603–25)					
	Charles I m. Henrietta Maria of France (r.1625–49)				Elizabeth m. Frederick, Elector Palatine, King of Bohemia	
Charles II m. Catherine (r.1660–85) of Braganza (no issue)	William II, m. Mary Prince of Orange	(1)Anne Hyde m. **James II** m. (2)Maria of Modena (r. 1685–8)		Rupert	Sophia m. Ernest Augustus, Elector of Hanover	
	William III m. **Mary II** (r.1689–1702) (r.1689–94)	**Anne** m. George (r.1702–14) of Denmark (no surviving issue)	James, Prince of Wales (The Old Pretender)	m. Clementina Sobieska	**George I** m. Sophia Dorothea (r.1714–27) of Celle	
Key r = reigned m = married				Charles Edward, Prince of Wales (d.1788) (The Young Pretender)		

18

Lady Nithsdale trying to make her handsome husband look like her friend Mrs Mills

handkerchief and walked out of the cell with the Countess to the neighbouring anteroom where the guards were chatting with their wives and daughters. None of them, hopefully, realised that Mrs. Mills was the same broken-hearted woman who had passed through minutes before. Their attention was on Lady Nithsdale as she spoke to her companion.

'Go in all haste and send me my waiting maid,' Lady Nithsdale begged. 'She certainly cannot reflect how late it is. I am to present my petition for my husband's release tonight and

ff I let slip this opportunity, I am undone, for tomorrow is too late!'

By this time, as Lady Nithsdale had fully intended, the comings and goings of Mrs. Mills had thoroughly confused the guards as to how many visitors had gone in and out of Lord Nithsdale's cell. The guards were also distracted from suspicions of trickery on Lady Nithsdale's part by the great sympathy they felt for this clearly desperate and distressed young wife. One guard was so affected that tears glistened in his eyes as he opened the door for Lady Nithsdale to return to her husband.

Once back in her husband's cell, Lady Nithsdale quickly completed her husband's disguise. When she had finished, the dark-haired, hand-some Earl, who had had no time to shave his beard, looked as much like Mrs. Mills as so short a time allowed. He seemed even more like her when he put a handkerchief to his face and began to sob into it, as she had, with piteous

19

wails and pathetic cries. Lady Nithsdale led him into the crowded anteroom with his head bent, still crying and mopping his eyes. The guards, now quite upset by the whole tragic affair, opened the door for the two of them. They made off down the stairs with Lord Nithsdale walking in front. His wife followed close behind to conceal the way her husband walked in his unfamiliar long gown. If one of the guards happened to notice his awkwardness,

he could well realise what had been going on.

The deception, however, was far from over. Once outside the Tower, Lord Nithsdale was hurried away to safety by Evans and Mr. Mills, and Lady Nithsdale returned up the stairs, complaining loudly about the continued ab-

Disguised, Lord Nithsdale escapes from his captors. Like many other Jacobites, he ended his days on foreign soil

sence of her maid. If she did not hurry, the Countess cried, it would be too late for her to present the petition for clemency which might save the Earl's life. The guards and their relatives nodded sympathetically and none of them noticed anything strange or cared to investigate when Lady Nithsdale went to her husband's cell and started up a conversation there.

Had anyone bothered to check, they would have found the Countess alone in the empty cell, pacing up and down in mock anxiety and 'conversing' with her husband by alternating her own voice with an imitation of his.

At length, Lady Nithsdale stood at the door of the cell and bade her husband a tearful farewell. Since the maid had not arrived, she 'told' him, she must go and present the petition for mercy herself. That done, Lady Nithsdale pulled the latch on the cell door so that it could not be opened from the outside, jammed it shut with some force and left. As she went, Lady Nithsdale tearfully told a guard that her husband was saying his prayers and should not be disturbed for several minutes.

By the time her elaborate ruse was discovered, Lady Nithsdale was well away from the Tower. Her husband got away from England in another disguise six days after his escape. Dressed as a footman to the Venetian ambassador, he travelled to Dover, where he took a small boat across the Channel. Later, he reached Rome, where he joined the Stuart royal family in exile. Lady Nithsdale followed him.

Neither of them ever returned home. Lord Nithsdale died in 1744, and his wife five years later; she had lived to see a second Jacobite Rebellion fail in 1745. However, the Nithsdales were not forgotten in England: the daring and enterprise of the escape was too thrilling for that to happen. At the time it occurred, the event even roused the admiration of King George I, who observed that it was 'the best thing a man in his condition could have done'. In his phlegmatic, unemotional fashion, King George was acknowledging what nearly all who have since heard the story have agreed upon: that the escape which Lady Nithsdale hatched with such ingenuity, performed with such aplomb and finally brought off with such verve was among the most dramatic the Tower of London has ever known.

CHAPTER 2

Freedom across the Border

*Minutes passed;
each seemed an hour to von Werra.
Then, he felt someone climbing
onto the Hurricane's wing.*

When Oberleutenant Franz von Werra of the Luftwaffe, the German air force, became a prisoner of war in September, 1940, his first thought was of escape. His next thought, however, was of the two daunting problems that faced any German trying to get out of a prison camp in wartime Britain.

First of all, since Britain was an island, there were no neutral countries bordering it where a prisoner on the run could find freedom. It was true that, after June 1940, the entire coastline of Europe opposite the British Isles was in German hands, but to get there, von Werra would first have to cross the English Channel. That was no small enterprise: with its violent moods, sudden storms and unpredictable currents, the Channel often contained more deadly perils than the open sea. Secondly, no German escaping from a POW camp could reckon that anyone outside was going to help him. Britain contained no Resistance workers with handy hideaways for him to shelter in, no-one to give him food, directions, arms or aid of any kind.

There was also a third bar against escaping – the conviction among Germans captured during 1940 that they only had to wait for the forces of the Third Reich to cross the Channel and overrun Britain. It seemed logical, after all. In May and June 1940, German forces had steamrollered to victory over Holland, Belgium and France in a matter of six weeks. The Dutch, Belgian and French armies had collapsed before the onslaught of German tanks and artillery and the pulverising blows dealt by the aircraft of the Luftwaffe. Britain had to be next. So what was the point of risking everything by trying to escape when rescue was so imminent?

When Franz von Werra arrived at Grizedale Hall, the stately home in the Lake District now being used as a prison camp, he heard much of this 'stay put and wait' argument, but he rejected it. Quite apart from the fact that it was the duty of every prisoner of war to escape, no matter how adverse the circumstances, von Werra was unconvinced that Britain would fall to German arms quite as easily as was generally imagined. The British, he knew, were a pig-headed nation, given to continuing a struggle long after logic indicated that they should have given up. As opponents, they were tough, tenacious, often ruthless – like the Spitfire pilot who crippled von Werra's aircraft on 5th September, 1940.

Franz von Werra trying to escape after crash landing his plane. He became one of several Luftwaffe pilots captured after the Battle of Britain

That day, the Battle of Britain was reaching the peak of its ferocity and von Werra's Messerschmitt 109 was one of several Luftwaffe planes locked in mammoth battle with Spitfires and Hurricanes in the brilliant blue, sunlit sky over Maidstone in Kent. Down below, people were watching as the combatants dived and roared about each other thousands of metres above, pumping out streams of machine gun fire and scarring the sky with exhaust fumes and the flames and smoke of crashing aircraft.

Suddenly, in the thick of the battle, von Werra felt his Messerschmitt judder as a Spitfire loosed a round of bullets into it. The Messerschmitt's engine spluttered, rallied, then spluttered again. Von Werra began to lose height and only just managed to sidle out of the way as another burst of fire came spitting towards him. By now the Messerschmitt was swooping earthwards at a rapidly increasing rate and soon, it was only 30 metres above the ground. Von Werra managed to level the plane out and just brushed across some treetops before he brought it slithering to a stop in a field, with the propeller blades gouging out great clumps of earth and hurling them high in the air. Quickly, he flung back the cockpit canopy and jumped out. He looked around him, thinking to make a run for it, only to see a group of armed British soldiers racing towards him.

23

Von Werra attempting to escape from an exercise party at Grizedale Hall

Three weeks later, Franz von Werra was taken to Grizedale Hall in the Lake District. Twelve days after that, on 7th October, he made his first attempt to escape.

That afternoon, von Werra was among a group of prisoners who marched out of the gates of Grizedale Hall to take their daily exercise. As they tramped along the country lane, armed soldiers watched them closely and an eagle-eyed sergeant rode up and down on a horse, checking and counting them. After a while, the prisoners came to a halt to take a brief rest. This was the moment von Werra had been waiting for; two of his fellow Germans draped a coat over a nearby wall, following a previously arranged plan. Casually, von Werra heaved himself up and stretched out on top of it. He closed his eyes, as if taking a doze, but through his half-shut eyelids he watched for other prisoners to signal that the guards were looking the other way. When the signal came, he rolled over the wall into a field.

Two women working in the field saw him and began frantically waving warnings to the guards. The prisoners cheered and waved back, as if in fun. The guards noticed nothing – yet.

Von Werra darted along the wall, plunged into some undergrowth and found himself in a small wood. He raced between the trees, up a steep incline, out across the fields beyond and then into more woods, running for almost two hours until he was satisfied he was not being followed.

Meanwhile, the guards had discovered they had one prisoner missing and a general hue and cry had begun. Troops were called out to comb the area, lorry loads of soldiers raced to all the likely points where von Werra might be found and the police forces of three counties turned out to scour the lakeland moors and hillsides for him. They searched and hunted hour after hour in pouring rain, but to no avail.

Then, on 10th October, three days after his escape, von Werra was discovered, dirty and dishevelled, in a stone shelter high up on a hill by two members of the Home Guard. Triumphantly, the two Home Guardsmen tied a rope round von Werra's right wrist and took him outside into the heavy rain. The three of them slid and slithered down a hillside awash with mud. In these conditions, the two captors were taken quite unawares when von Werra suddenly pulled on the rope, toppling them over into the mud and putting out the lamp they were carrying. Taking advantage of the sudden pitch darkness, von Werra scrambled up the slippery hillside and vanished.

The two Guardsmen began a frantic search but, hindered by the rain teeming down in thick curtains, they could find no trace of him. However, von Werra's luck was not to last out much longer in these harrowing conditions; exhausted, hungry and unable to run any further, he took shelter in a field near Eskdale. There, a local farmer caught sight of him and signalled to a group of soldiers who were hunting for the escaper on the next hill. When, finally, they caught up with von Werra and pulled him out of a bog, he was sodden, shivering, plastered in mud from head to foot and almost unconscious from extreme fatigue.

Von Werra, undeterred, spent his punishment period – three weeks' solitary confinement – planning his next attempt to get away. His plans received a setback, however, when he discovered that he was being transferred to a more secure prison camp – The Hayes at Swanwick near Derby. Unlike Grizedale Hall, The Hayes was an integral camp and included plenty of space for prisoners to take their exercise within the barbed wire. There would be no slipping off during country walks.

After his second unsuccessful attempt at escape, von Werra is rescued from a bog

Von Werra's final attempt to escape from England is foiled. No POW ever succeeded

Von Werra's solution, after careful reconnaissance of the grounds, was the escaper's familiar standby – a tunnel. He formed a team with four other prisoners and on 17th November, 1940, they removed a square of parquet flooring in one of the prison camp rooms and started to dig. The digging proceeded slowly and painfully, undetected by the British, and often at the risk of the tunnellers' lives. Many times, they emerged from clawing their way through the underground clay gasping from lack of air and covered in grime and mud. On 17th December, exactly a month after it had started, the escape tunnel emerged outside the barbed wire, at a point which, luckily, was hidden by a hedge.

A few days later, a stranger dressed in a flying suit presented himself at Hucknall R.A.F. Aerodrome, about 12 kilometres southeast of The Hayes. Speaking good English but with a thick accent, he said he was Captain van Lott, a Dutch airman serving with Coastal Command. His Wellington bomber had crashed and he wanted help to get back to base at Dyce Airfield, near Aberdeen. Van Lott was, of course, Franz von Werra. Together with his four companions – all of whom were quickly recaptured – he had wriggled out of the tunnel across the tarmac, he reached a hangar where he told a mechanic that he had just arrived at Hucknall. Could he take a Hurricane fighter up for a practice flight?

The mechanic believed him, or appeared to, and after some delay allowed von Werra to climb into the cockpit of a Hurricane that was standing nearby. The Hurricane's controls were completely strange to von Werra and he had to sit there, edgy with nerves, while the mechanic explained them. The mechanic then went off to fetch an accumulator to charge the aircraft's engine. Minutes passed; each seemed an hour to von Werra. Then, he felt someone climbing onto the Hurricane's wing. He turned round. It was the duty officer who had made the telephone call to Aberdeen; in his hand, only a hair's-breadth away from von Werra's face, was a revolver.

No German prisoner of war ever succeeded in escaping from wartime Britain, not even the daredevil Franz von Werra. And none, of course, was rescued by any invading German army. In October 1940, with the R.A.F. victorious in the Battle of Britain, Adolf Hitler had been forced to postpone his attack 'indefinitely'. Then, in 1941, von Werra and other Germans who had made attempts to escape suffered a depressing blow to their hopes of any further chances: their captors began to ship them across the Atlantic to prison camps in Canada.

Franz von Werra sailed for Canada with over 1,000 other German prisoners on 10th January, 1941. By the time the long ocean voyage was over and his ship, *Duchess of York*, had berthed at Halifax, Nova Scotia, he had already worked out an idea for his next escape. Despite its enormous distance from Germany and home, Canada offered one great advantage as escape country: it bordered the United States, which at that time was still neutral. What was more, the train taking the prisoners to their camp on the north shore of Lake Ontario was likely to travel close to the frontier for part of the way.

The train rolled over the snow-covered winter landscape, taking the Germans deeper and deeper into the heart of Canada. Tedious days passed. Von Werra spent the time surreptitiously freeing the outside window of a double pair of windows from its encrusting of

after dark on 20th December. By the time he reached Hucknall Aerodrome under his bogus Dutch name, von Werra, had spent many hair-raising hours dodging the police and undergoing exacting cross-examinations from a highly suspicious local stationmaster and three plain clothes detectives. Somehow he managed to survive their close questioning without being unmasked, and he even got the authorities at Hucknall to send a car to pick him up.

Von Werra was taken to the duty officer's hut at the aerodrome, where he was told to wait while his identity was checked with his supposed base at Aberdeen. The telephone call would take only a few minutes and his story would, naturally, be revealed as false. Von Werra therefore had only those few minutes in which to get away, and he planned to do so by audacious means – by stealing an aircraft from one of the hangars. He made an excuse to get out of the duty officer's hut while the man was still on the line to Aberdeen. Walking quickly thick ice. At last, the ice yielded and he managed to wedge the window open. That evening, as the train pulled out of Montreal station, he snuggled down in his thick coat as if to go to sleep. Furtively, with eyes half closed, he edged up to the window. A few minutes later, another prisoner, Leutenant Wagner, shook out his blanket in the centre of the carriage, obscuring von Werra for a few vital moments from the guard on watch outside. In that flash of time, von Werra heaved up the double panes and flung himself head first out of the window. The icy winter blasts hit him full in the face as he tumbled onto the side of the track and landed in a pile of thick snow.

As the train drew away into the darkness and vanished from sight, von Werra set off on a gruelling trudge through deep snowdrifts. He struggled through a dense forest in pitch blackness and reached the road that led to the north bank of the St. Lawrence River. Starving, exhausted and numb with cold he somehow managed to keep on going until eventually he reached the river. There, he caught his first sight of free territory for four months – lights twinkling among some houses on the other, American, side of the river.

Von Werra's first idea was to crawl over the frozen river surface, but after creeping forward a short distance, he found it was not frozen the whole way across. He stumbled back to the Canadian shore. Almost immediately his attention was caught by a mound of snow and on

investigation, he found that this was concealing the one thing he most needed – a small boat. Luck was with him at last. Von Werra battled to free the boat, then pushed it over the frozen St. Lawrence to the point where a stream of water separated the sheets of ice on either side. He shouldered the boat into the water, fell into it and let the current take it down river until it bumped against the ice on the opposite side.

Almost fainting with fatigue and cold, von Werra crawled out of the boat onto the ice and dragged himself over to the river bank. With enormous effort, he heaved himself up on his feet and stumbled away. For hours, it seemed, he waded through the snow. Then, he reached a dark, desolate forest, groped his way through and, just as dawn was brightening the sky, he came upon a road. Von Werra was some way down the road when he saw a car. It had broken down and the driver and his companion were hovering anxiously near the open bonnet. Von Werra staggered up to them. Their eyes opened wide as they viewed him with astonishment: the German was a terrible sight, covered in snow and thoroughly dishevelled with his ears a frostbitten blue, and he was asking the most ludicrous of questions.

'Is this America?' he gasped.

The astonished couple assured him it was.

In spite of the Arctic conditions, freedom for von Werra is within reach across the border

He was near Ogdensburg in New York State, they said.

'In that case,' von Werra told them in weary but triumphant tones, 'I am an officer of the German Air Force. I have escaped across the river from Canada. I am . . .' von Werra paused, 'I *was* a prisoner of war!'

The last photograph of von Werra to appear in the German press. He wears the much coveted decoration of the Knight's Cross of the Iron Cross awarded him in January 1941

CHAPTER 3

From the Cocos to Constantinople

*Hurriedly, the Germans
hurled themselves behind some rocks,
expecting that at any moment, the
Bedouins would open fire.*

The fifty German sailors standing on the palm-fringed shore of Direction Island in the Cocos Islands could hardly believe what they were seeing on Sunday, 9th November, 1914. Their ship, the 3,000 tonne cruiser *Emden* was sailing without them. The German contingent, whose leader, Helmut von Mucke, was second in command of *Emden*, watched with amazement as the cruiser moved away towards the horizon, its stern growing smaller and smaller to their view. An awesome fact dawned: they were marooned. And, what was more, marooned on an island controlled by Britain, the country they had been fighting since the First World War had begun three months earlier.

The Cocos Islands were extremely remote – they were situated in the Indian Ocean, 2,750 kilometres north-west of Australia – but war was war even in such an isolated outpost of the British Empire. Helmut von Mucke was well aware that he and his men could all be made prisoners, all the more certainly because they had come ashore on Direction Island to wreck the wireless station there. They had, in fact, already started their work of destruction when they saw the *Emden* leaving.

Mucke narrowed his eyes and gazed out to sea to watch the rapidly disappearing ship. Captain von Muller, its commander, would never have weighed anchor like that and left part of his crew stranded unless he had good reason for doing so. Before long, as he followed *Emden* with his eyes, Mucke saw what that reason was. Another ship, an enemy, the 6,000 tonne Australian cruiser *Sydney*, was closing on *Emden* at speed, guns blazing. It was a sinister experience, standing in serene, sunlit surroundings on a warm, soft sand beach witnessing a fight to the death as massive naval guns spat flames and smoke, shooting at each other across the water.

The stranded German sailors unknowingly watch the destruction of their ship Emden

The captain and crew of *Sydney* must be feeling triumphant, Mucke reflected. *Emden* had been at large in the Indian Ocean for several weeks, preying on enemy shipping and causing such havoc that trade around the coast of India had had to be suspended. Every British and Allied ship in the ocean was on the lookout for the marauding German. Now *Sydney* had at last caught up with her, the Australians were going to do their best to make sure she did not escape. Mucke and his men saw the two ships vanish from sight over the horizon, still firing great broadsides at each other. Later, at the end of November, Mucke was to learn that the contest had ended with the destruction of the *Emden*.

As he stood on the shore, Mucke realised that he must get his men away from the Cocos Islands, and quickly. The only way out was by sea, but the ship the Germans found after scouring the shores of Direction Island was hardly suitable. The rusting, dilapidated, neglected old sailing schooner *Ayesha* had not tasted the

waters of the Indian Ocean for years. Her hull was peppered with holes, her sails shabby and torn. She was nothing but a leaky hulk, but she would have to do.

That same evening, after patching *Ayesha* as best they could, the 50 Germans set sail and headed the schooner's prow towards the reefs. At any moment, they were sure, she would start capsizing, but by some miracle, the old schooner cleared the reefs and stood out to sea.

In the next three weeks, monsoons and storms whipped up huge waves around *Ayesha* and mighty winds tore along her open deck and sliced huge tears in her old sails. Many of the Germans, crammed into deck space meant for only five men, heartily wished they had remained on Direction Island, even if it did mean imprisonment for the rest of the war. Better that than sinking and drowning in the vast and violent ocean. Somehow, though, *Ayesha* kept afloat until, at last, land came in sight. It was Sumatra, a Dutch island colony and therefore neutral territory. Joyously, Mucke steered *Ayesha* towards the harbour at Pedang where he saw, to his added delight, several German merchant ships lying at anchor.

As soon as he went ashore at Pedang, however, one grim fact became clear: the Dutch might be neutral in the First World War, but they were not friendly to Germans. But Mucke and his men had not survived such harrowing experiences at sea in order to suffer internment at the hands of the Dutch. To avoid it, Mucke made secret arrangements with the captain of a German steamer at Pedang, and only 24 hours after arriving in harbour there, he took *Ayesha* out to sea again.

The Dutch were relieved, but were convinced that the Germans were intent on committing suicide. They would be washed ashore sometime on one of the scattered Indian Ocean islands or would disappear for ever in the depths of the sea. In actual fact, Mucke was carrying out the secret plan he had hatched at Pedang. It came to fruition two weeks later when the captain of the German steamer arrived at a point some distance down the coast to rendezvous with *Ayesha*. By that time, Mucke had managed to avoid three enemy ships who were searching for the fugitives from *Emden*, as well as the British cruiser *Himalaya*.

The Germans boarded the steamer and stood on deck watching as *Ayesha* capsized where they had scuttled her. Her cracked old hull, battered masts and torn sails slowly disappeared as the sea closed over them and she sank to the ocean bed. Mucke sighed. It was a very sad thing to see a valiant old vessel go down like that, particularly a ship that had secured liberty for himself and his fellow crewmen.

That liberty, however, was by no means completely won yet. Fifty Germans could not just go island hopping across the Indian Ocean looking for a safe place to shelter. There were too many British colonies there and too many British ships still hunting for them. The only way to make escape complete was to make for the nearest friendly territory. 'Nearest' hardly seemed an appropriate term to describe Arabia, a colony of the Turks who were Germany's allies in the war, for Arabia lay north-westwards across no less than 6,750 kilometres of ocean. Fortunately, though, the Pedang steamer was a sturdy little ship and accomplished this long voyage without trouble. Mucke and his men disembarked at the Arabian port of Hodeida and bade farewell to the captain and crew of the German steamer. It was at Hodeida, however, that the trouble really began.

The Germans discovered to their alarm that the town was occupied by enemies, in the form of French troops. There was even a large French cruiser moored in the harbour. Mucke was appalled. Again, he was stranded, for there was nowhere else he could go. There was nothing for it but for him to get his men ashore in secret by night and try to cross the desert to where the French could not touch them.

As soon as it got dark, Mucke piloted the steamer close inshore, floated out small boats and rowed through the heavy surf for the beach. The Germans started to scramble up the

sand, scanning the darkness for signs that they were being watched. They had just decided, to their relief, that their landing had gone unobserved when they saw the Bedouins. Bedouin tribesmen – scores of them – were standing a few metres away, glaring fixedly at them. For a moment, seeing their red and blue uniforms, Mucke feared they were part of the French forces. Hurriedly, the Germans grabbed their kit from the boats and hurled themselves behind some rocks, expecting that at any moment,

Bedouin tribesmen confront the Germans as they attempt to land silently on the beach

Helmut von Mucke

the Bedouins would open fire. To Mucke's intense relief, not a shot rang out. The Bedouins' wariness vanished inexplicably and they turned quite friendly. They even insisted on accompanying the Germans on their journey inland.

Mucke and his men had not gone far, however, before they learned dispiriting news. A column of Turkish cavalry they encountered told them that the only way to reach the safety they sought was to march across the mountains to Saana, capital of Yemen. The prospect was daunting. It meant seven or eight weeks of climbing mountains 3,500 metres high, where the air was so thin it made breathing difficult and freezing frosts and snow lay on the stone-strewn paths. But it was either that long, gruelling slog or put to sea again, where some British or French ship was bound to intercept and capture them. So, the Germans set off on their mammoth trek through the mountains. By the time they reached Saana they were tattered and

utterly exhausted. To their fury, they quickly discovered that this supposedly 'safe' town was in fact full of perils.

Arabian rebels were limbering up to attack Saana at any moment and the Turks there refused to let Mucke have any camels to get away. The wily Turks had their eyes on the four Maxim machine guns the Germans had brought with them: very useful against a horde of wild tribesmen. Mucke was infuriated. He had no intention of fighting the Turks' battles for them, even if they *were* allies of Germany. If they would not help, Mucke decided, he would get the camels he needed from their opponents. The Arabian tribesmen drove a difficult bargain and Mucke had to haggle hard to get them to agree to a deal. But eventually, for a very

After an exhausting journey across the desert von Mucke's hopes are dashed. The boat lies rotten and half submerged beneath the waves

stiff price, the Arabians let Mucke buy camels for the journey down to the Red Sea.

Mucke's destination was a point along the coast where a friendly Turkish engineer in Saana had told him there was a government-owned launch lying at anchor. Anxious to reach the launch as soon as possible to check its seaworthiness, Mucke rode on ahead, remaining in the saddle without sleep or much food for three days and nights. He arrived on the coast with his hair and skin caked by sand

blown up by desert winds and his body sagging with fatigue to be greeted by the very worst sight imaginable. He nearly burst into tears when he saw the launch on which he had pinned so much hope. It reminded him of *Ayesha*, only worse. All he could see of the boat was the upper part of its funnel, the rest was lying rotten and submerged beneath the water.

Mucke was plunged into despair, but all the same he refused to give up. When the rest of his men arrived at the coast, he ordered them to ride back inland for a day and there await further orders. Then, he set off for Hodeida. He scoured the town, always on the lookout for French troops who might try to arrest him, until he found an Arabian who had two small sailing boats lying at anchor in a bay north of Hodeida. Mucke bribed the man to let him use the boats and then sent word to his men to get to the bay with all speed. When they came riding in from the desert, he packed them into the craft and set sail.

It was a highly hazardous journey; many of the Germans were already sick and suffering from dysentery, malaria and typhoid before they set sail. To make matters worse, Mucke had no charts and the incompetent Arab pilot he had hired ran the first boat onto a reef. A heavy sea was running at the time and it was only by incredible good fortune that the boat managed to get free and float out to safer water. The second boat, which carried the sick, was less lucky. It met the spiky coral full on, splintered apart and foundered.

The Germans on board were tossed into the heaving sea, which was infested with sharks, and lost in the darkness. Mucke took the enormous risk of firing off some flares, which he had brought with him from the *Emden*. As they speared up into the sky and sparkled white and bright over the scene, they could be spotted far into the distance. Their light picked out the Germans struggling in the water and enabled all of them to be hauled to safety in the first boat. Mucke was thankful when the task was over and the flares had fizzled out.

However, as a result, everything that could be abandoned, except for the arms and ammunition and a mere two days' supply of food and water, was jettisoned so that the small boat with its greatly increased load did not sink. Even when the boat had been lightened as much as possible its gunwale was a dangerous 45 centimetres above the water's surface; a sudden wave or heavy sea could swamp it in seconds. Then came a stroke of luck. The wind turned from an adverse northerly to a favourable southerly, and at last, the Germans managed to reach land safely.

They stumbled ashore, thankful just to be alive. Mucke, anxious to move on, managed to obtain some camels from a friendly Arab sheik and they set off northwards across the desert towards the Turkish fortress of Djidda. Not far from Djidda, a wild tribe of Bedouins suddenly opened fire at them from behind some sand dunes. The Germans dismounted quickly

and ran for cover, the 25 men who were still fit and well dragging or carrying their sick companions. Hastily, they set up their machine guns and began firing back. It was a long and vicious battle – three day and nights of hectic fighting in sweltering temperatures of around 55°C. At long last, and just before sand jammed up the machine gun mechanisms, the Germans managed to break through the

The struggling sailors being hauled to safety from the dangers of the shark infested waters

Bedouin ambush and escape. But the cost had been appalling: several Germans were dead, many were wounded and most of the camels, their sole source of transport, had been killed. When the survivors reached Djidda, Mucke decided they would all be safer at sea than in the unfriendly, Bedouin-infested desert.

They took possession of a boat which they found at Djidda harbour and set sail, creeping along the coast between the coral reefs and keeping a wary eye open for signs of enemies. They had one narrow escape when they saw a gunboat that seemed to be searching the shore-line for them; as it passed by, the German boat lay hidden among the coral reefs and managed to remain undetected.

That gunboat was the last enemy the Ger-mans encountered on their long and gruelling escape. They sailed on to the coast of northern Arabia, where they landed and managed to reach the southern end of the Syrian railway. They were in truly friendly territory at last. A few weeks later, in June 1915, Helmut von Mucke walked into the offices of the German naval authorities in Constantinople, capital of the Ottoman Turkish Empire. There, he pre-sented officials with the flag of his lost ship, the *Emden*. He had carried it with him for seven months, across thousands of kilometres of ocean, burning desert and freezing mountain ranges and through more perils that most men could pack into a lifetime.

CHAPTER 4

Rescue from Libby Prison

*The prisoner breathed
a sigh of relief and blessed the
rodent inhabitants of the cellar; until now,
he had never thought he would come to
regard rats as his friends.*

There was something sinister about Libby prison, in Richmond, Virginia. Second Lieutenant James Wells of the 8th Michigan Cavalry could feel its grim atmosphere enveloping him as he stood with other Northern – Unionist – prisoners at the entrance, awaiting admission. Wells felt depressed and utterly weary. It had been a long, gruelling march from Mouse Creek, where he had been captured by Southern – Confederate – forces on 23rd September, 1863. The 150 kilometres of tramping over rough ground, fording swift running rivers and being tossed around in small boats had given him plenty of time to realise that in this dreadful civil war, which had torn the United States in two since 1861, the Confederates who had once been his fellow countrymen had now become his jailers.

After such a dispiriting and exhausting journey, Wells felt almost glad that he had at least reached a place where he could lie down and sleep – even if it *was* the bleak and dismal Libby prison. Suddenly, he sensed eyes watching him. He glanced up to the prison windows. There, behind thick bars of iron, he glimpsed the pale, scrawny faces of the inmates. They were watching the scene below with gaunt gaze and in that moment, Wells was able to believe the rumours he had heard about prisoners going mad at Libby, or trying to kill themselves.

Once inside the prison, it quickly became even more apparent to Wells that there was truth in the rumours. Close to, the inmates already there seemed drained of hope and energy. They were haggard, hungry and weak and had slept on nothing but bare stone floors since they arrived. They were also nearly hysterical in their anxiety for news. As soon as Wells and the other new prisoners appeared, they were besieged with questions. How was the war going? Was the Unionist North winning its struggle to free the Negro slaves and stop the southerners setting up their own independent country? Or was the Confederate South winning *its* fight to maintain that independence and keep slaves to cultivate their cotton and other plantations? There were floods of personal questions, too. Did Wells know how their families were faring? Were they safe? Were they alive? Had their homes been destroyed in some battle, or were they still intact?

One thing was significant, though, and James Wells soon noticed it. The men who kept in the best spirits and the best health were not those consumed by such anxieties. They were the ones who prowled round the prison, examining the walls, the floors, the entrances, looking anywhere and everywhere for some means of escape. In these circumstances, escape was not just a desire to be free of the shame and frustration of captivity. It was a way of keeping sane and maintaining the will to survive.

Libby Prison was renowned as one of the grimmest prisons in the South. 60,000 soldiers died in prison camps during the war

Cross section of the escape route from Libby Prison. Escaping prisoners nearly suffocated from the rank air inside the narrow tunnel

Naturally, prisoners engaged on constant reconnaissance of the prison got to know one another quite well. By the end of 1863, fifteen of them, James Wells included, had got together to plan a mass escape, which they intended to make possible by digging a tunnel. The tunnel, they planned, would start in a fireplace in one of the prison rooms, travel down for about a metre inside a partition wall and then emerge through the same wall into a cellar them with soot and ashes to stop the guards noticing they were loose. The escape end, in the carriage shed, possessed a high fence which screened it from the view of prison guards.

Work began one night around Christmas 1863 when about 75 bricks were furtively removed from the fireplace, leaving enough room for one man to crawl through and down the partition wall until he reached the cellar. Taking it in turns to work shifts during the night, the tunnellers cleared a way through the bottom of the cellar and then, watched by an audience of cellar rats, commenced serious digging. Night after night for seven weeks, they scraped and clawed away at the earth with clam shells and small knives until a tunnel 40 centimetres wide and running about three metres below the ground began to move out underneath the street outside the prison. The earth they dug out was hidden by clearing aside some of the straw stacked in the cellar, scattering the soil evenly over the floor and then spreading the straw back over it.

However, as the tunnel grew longer, the air inside it became increasingly foul. By the time six metres – one third of the tunnel – had been dug, prisoners were emerging blue in the face from lack of air and retching from the vileness of it. James Wells later remarked that the putrid stink inside the tunnel remained in his nostrils for many months afterwards. To overcome the problem, one man fanned the tunnel entrance in the cellar to drive fresher air inside it, while another dug out more earth.

For weeks, the clandestine burrowing went on until Wells and the other escapers decided to test how far across the street the tunnel had reached. This piece of prospecting was done with a chisel and it very nearly put an end to the whole venture. When one of the prisoners pushed the chisel up through the roof of the tunnel, it emerged with a clattering noise above the ground, right next to a street lamp. The noise alerted two guards on patrol.

'Hear that?' said one.

'Oh, it's only rats!' his companion replied.

The prisoner, crouching below and listening in trepidation, breathed a huge sigh of relief and blessed the rodent inhabitants of the cellar; until now, he had never thought he would come to regard rats as his friends.

beneath the eastern end of the building. From there, the tunnellers planned to dig a way out eastwards under the street so as to emerge in a carriage shed that stood on the opposite side. The starting end of the tunnel would be disguised while work was in progress by replacing bricks taken from the fireplace and dirtying

The prospecting had revealed that there was still at least five metres of tunnel to be dug before the floor of the carriage shed was reached and it was not until early in February 1864, after nearly two months' work, that the last short stretch was excavated. The last tunneller poked his head out to reconnoitre and saw to his delight that the tunnel was well inside the shed and completely screened from the guards.

On the night of 9th February, 1864, a mass of escapers began to gather round the fireplace at the entrance to the tunnel. The bricks were removed and one by one, they squeezed themselves through the hole and down into the cellar, then wriggled along under the street until they clambered out into the carriage shed covered in mud and gasping from the vile air.

A contemporary engraving of Richmond, the capital of both the state of Virginia and the Confederacy

James Wells was the fifteenth man through. He dragged his coat out of the tunnel after him, shook off the clods of mud clinging to it, then moved swiftly towards the gate that led to the street outside. Wells waited until the guard who was pacing back and forth along the street had turned his back, then he nipped swiftly through the gate and along the pavement in the opposite direction.

On that February night in the third year of

the American Civil War, James Wells was one of 109 Unionist prisoners who escaped from Libby prison through the tunnel. Forty-eight got clean away and though James Wells was among them, there were many moments when it looked as if he would join the unlucky majority who were recaptured.

The first thing he had to do was to get out of Richmond, and get out quickly. As soon as the escape was discovered, the Confederates would start hunting the prisoners with dogs. Keeping well away from street lamps, Wells made his way towards the outskirts of Richmond, where he had to get past a guard post and some fortifications. He managed to escape detection as he passed the guard post, but the fortifications posed a tricky problem. For an hour, Wells crawled along on all fours right up against the high walls while, directly above him, sentries stood guard on the parapets. One glance down was all it needed for Wells to be spotted. But all went well: no-one saw him and Wells was at last clear of the wall and able to contemplate the broad sweep of open Virginia countryside that lay beyond Richmond.

It was now close to dawn, and after fording a deep, fast-flowing stream, Wells bedded down in a thicket where he planned to hide while the daylight hours passed. Around mid-morning, the sound of horses reached his ears. Poking his head above the thicket, Wells was just in time to see a troop of Confederate cavalry riding past. Swiftly, he ducked down. The cavalry passed on, but Wells had guessed what they were doing – they were searching for the escaped prisoners.

As soon as it got dark again, he left the thicket and tramped through the night until he found a signpost on the road that told him he had travelled 20 kilometres from Richmond. This far, he had been lucky to remain unseen and undetected, but then, only a short while after blessing his good fortune, Wells walked straight into danger. Suddenly, he found himself in the middle of a Confederate army encampment; it was ringed by thick woodlands and impossible to scout around, so the only thing he could do was to go through it.

Confederate soldiers were busying themselves about the camp getting the mules and wagons ready to move off when day came.

Wells decided that the best thing for him to do was to emulate them – shout orders at the mules and heave at the wagons and generally pretend to be part of their troop. A mule stood quite close by, gazing at him with mournful eyes, so Wells walked up to it, yelled a sharp command in its long ear and moved on. Several more mules got the same treatment and for good measure, Wells gave one or two a shove in the ribs to emphasise his commands. At last, he reached the edge of the encampment. As soon as he was sure no-one was watching, he hared off into the shrubbery, his heart thumping at his own impudence and at his luck. Soon afterwards, as daylight filtered through the trees, Wells crawled into a hiding place to await another night.

Sixteen hours later, just as he was preparing to move on, he heard a twig crack. Someone was coming. Wells held his breath as he crouched still and tense inside his hiding place. The dim outlines of two men appeared, but as they came closer, Wells recognised them. They were two of his fellow escapers from Libby prison – McCain and Randall.

McCain and Randall started when they heard a hiss and a hoarse whisper coming from behind a nearby bush. But they were overjoyed when they found it was Wells. Wells, for his part, was equally pleased to see them. To his delight

The three escaped Yankees watching and hiding from the Confederate cavalry

diers of the Unionist army, who were fighting to obtain freedom for slaves like themselves, gave the fugitives food and even spied out the land for them in case Confederate pursuers were about.

Then, on Sunday 17th February, eight days after the escape began, Wells, McCain and Randall reached the edge of the woods and found themselves on the outskirts of a small township. Keeping well out of sight behind a pile of brushwood, they watched the people going to church. Then, suddenly, the sound of horses' hooves reached their ears: 75 Confederate cavalrymen went riding by only a few metres from where they lay. At the same time, some small dogs came racing towards their hiding place yapping and barking, but to their relief, before anyone could come up to investigate, something else caught the dogs' attention and they scampered off to nose around among some trees a short distance away.

At that point Randall decided to crawl down towards the road that ran through the town to see if he could find a path by which they could

they had some food which they offered him – not much, just a few crusts of corn bread, but it was the first food Wells had had for 36 hours and it tasted as good as a banquet.

After that, the three escapers set off together, but four nights later, they were so exhausted that they were stumbling through the night and collapsing utterly spent into a hideout by day. Had it not been for the Negroes they met on the way, they would probably never have survived. The Negroes, recognising them as sol-

45

get away without being detected. Moments after he disappeared into the bushes, however, three or four shots rang out followed by a loud yell. Wells and McCain waited, hoping Randall would return. A few more minutes passed but there was no sign of him. Sadly, Wells and McCain realised that Randall must have been shot and killed.

Suddenly, one of the small dogs came pelting back, burst through the brush and confronted them, barking so hard that it bounced up and down on the ground. Wells and McCain started up at once and ran. Within moments, they were spotted. Cavalrymen came clattering and pounding after them, and it was only by dodging back into thickets and dense woods where horses could not follow, that the two of them managed to get away.

Still fearful of pursuit, however, they plunged neck deep into a swamp in the woods and hid there until night returned. When darkness fell, the two men dragged themselves out and pressed on. Fortunately, they soon

came upon a cabin whose lone inhabitant was able to offer the starving men some dry biscuits to eat. He also gave them some encouraging news. From what he told them, Wells and McCain realised they were close to Williamsburg and at Williamsburg, they knew, a contingent of their own, Unionist, troops was stationed.

About a week later, Wells and McCain were crouching in some undergrowth by the road that led, or so they believed, to Williamsburg. If they were not quite sure where they were it was not surprising. The previous seven days had been the worst and most debilitating of the whole escape, full of raging storms, sleet, driving rain and winds so strong that at times they threatened to rip the clothes from their backs. The two men were ragged, wet through and aching inside with hunger. Wells found that the long days of effort and deprivation were beginning to affect his memory; he spent some hours struggling to remember the name of his only brother.

Then, just as he and McCain were debating in whispers whether they were near Williamsburg or not, they heard cavalry. Confederates again? Or Unionist cavalry? As he listened, a ray of hope dawned in Wells's befuddled mind. The horsemen's sabres were rattling inside iron scabbards. Confederate cavalry did not carry sabres. Wells communicated this news to McCain, and they decided to risk it and show themselves. As the cavalry rode by, they swayed to their feet and feebly waved their arms. 'What regiment are you?' Wells called out hoarsely.

The cavalrymen wheeled about immediately, drew their pistols and yelled: 'Surrender! Give yourselves up or we shoot!' For one horrible moment, Wells was sure he had made a dreadful mistake.

'Who are you?' he cried out, expecting to hear the name of some Confederate regiment. But the reply, when it came, brought tears of relief to his eyes.

'11th Pennsylvania Cavalry!' the Northern Unionist horsemen shouted back. 'Some of our men have escaped from Libby prison at Richmond. We're a rescue party. Would you by any chance want rescuing?'

Luck favours the escapers as they run into their own Pennsylvania Cavalry

CHAPTER 5

Escape from Colditz

After two hours of shivering in dark discomfort, Larive and Steinmetz decided that the Germans were not going to discover the well.

It was stifling inside the well. The air was foul and heavy with the dank, iron smell of near-stagnant water. The two Dutchmen knew that if they had to remain down there for too long, they would probably be overcome by it, if, that is, they hadn't choked to death first from lack of oxygen. Already, after two hours in hiding, waiting for the Colditz Castle guards to stop looking for them. E. H. Larive and Francis Steinmetz were suffering acute symptoms of suffocation: violent, stabbing headaches, misty vision and lungs that ached as they fought for breath.

Larive peered up in the grey dimness of the well at the square of cement that covered it. If he could just lift it, even a few centimetres, he and Steinmetz could get some air from outside. But of course, there were risks. One of the guards searching for them in the park above might happen to notice the top side of the concrete slab moving as Larive pushed it, or he might hear it scrape. That would certainly be the end of the escape. It would be back to confinement in Colditz and days, maybe weeks, in the punishment block.

Distasteful visions of all this flashed across Larive's mind in that moment. The next moment, another image arose – of himself and Steinmetz dying in the well, gasping their lives away like fish on land. That decided it. Larive crawled slowly up the iron ladder that lined the well, pushed the slab up slightly and stuck his penknife in the aperture to keep it open. It was enough to let the precious fresh air seep in.

With the flow of air came a shaft of daylight, only a glimmer, but enough to reveal that the August sky was still bright and it would be some hours before dusk. In fact, another six hours had to pass before it would be dark enough to make a run for it, with any real hope of getting away and remaining free sufficiently long to reach neutral territory across the Swiss border. The two Dutchmen, feeling somewhat better now, settled back on the iron ladder to wait for the tedious hours to pass.

Colditz, made famous by countless escape tales, is an awesome medieval castle

It took patience as well as nerve to be successful in a prison camp escape. That was particularly true when it came to escaping from Colditz Castle, the camp which the Germans sent prisoners to when they had proved tiresome through their addiction to escape elsewhere.

The imposing medieval castle set on a hill above Colditz village, in upper Saxony, was an ideal place in which to keep difficult prisoners confined. It had high stone walls, courtyards

49

ringed by towers, turrets and lofty buildings, and an uninterrupted view of the surrounding countryside. Nowhere did the Germans guard their prisoners of war more strongly or with such a show of armed might than they did here. Rifles, bayonets and machine guns were constantly in evidence. So were powerful searchlights. Microphones were planted all over the castle to pick up furtive conversations. Roll calls were frequent. The Germans censored the prisoners' mail. They took their fingerprints, photographed them, kept meticulous files on them and planted guards at every corner, by every wall and on every battlement and terrace. Living in Colditz was a claustrophobic experience for everyone there – the more than 500 prisoners and their guards alike.

Colditz Castle had become a prisoner-of-war camp in October 1939, about a month after the start of the Second World War and almost two years before Lieutenant E. H. Larive of the Royal Netherlands Navy was sent there. Larive's background was similar to that of all the other inmates at Colditz: he had escaped from his first camp, Oflag 6A Soest, in September 1940 and managed to remain at liberty for nearly two weeks, getting to within metres of the Swiss border before he was caught. His next camp, near Breslau, failed to change him; he became involved in what the Germans considered 'suspicious' activities to do with escape and once attempted to walk through the gates in civilian clothes.

Larive was now labelled as a 'bad type' and an 'undesirable', the sort of prisoner who should be sent to Colditz. The Germans had the chance to realise that a lot earlier than they did, on 15th July, 1940 the day Larive refused to sign a formal pledge not to fight against the Nazi Reich or harm it in any way. The pledge had been the Germans' way of putting a final touch of humiliation to their conquest of Holland two months earlier when, within four days, their armies had blasted the Dutch into surrender with tanks, artillery and murderous air attacks. Refusing to sign was Lieutenant Larive's way of refusing to bow to such a barbaric invasion. He was not the only one. Sixty-seven other Dutch officers, including Francis Steinmetz, felt the same way and refused to sign the 'vile' and 'infernal' document.

Next day, Larive, Steinmetz and the rest were taken to barracks in Amsterdam and a few days later were being shunted by train to prison camps in Germany. Larive was taken to Colditz Castle a year afterwards. At the very moment he walked in, he was already thinking about escape and had brought with him two indispensable aids: money and a compass. The compass he had hidden inside a tin of apple syrup and the money was in his clothes. Spot checks at the gate when Larive arrived failed to detect either.

Colditz, Larive quickly discovered, was a 'think tank' of escape plans and during the War, some 300 escapes, 30 of them successful, were made from this supposedly secure fortress. The whole place seethed with talk of escape and the devices and deceptions that could help accomplish it.

At the hub of all this plotting was a Netherlands East Indies Army officer, Captain Chiel van den Heuvel; a selfless man of great enterprise, he had abandoned his own attempts at escape in order to help his fellow prisoners to do so. It was van den Heuval who first noticed the slab of cement about one metre square set flush in the grass of the park where prisoners took their exercise. Thousands of times prisoners had strolled past it, sat on it and looked at it without realising its possibilities. Van den Heuvel called some of them over, and they sat round the slab, apparently chatting, but in reality concealing it from the watchful guards while van den Heuvel lifted it a few centimetres to see what was underneath. It was a well, around three metres deep, half filled with water: an ideal, if dank, hiding place.

At once, the well was noted as a potential means of escape from Colditz Castle. Two officers of the Netherlands East Indies Army, Captain Dufour and Lieutenant Smit, were the first to use it; on 13th August 1941, they hid there while other prisoners kept their absence secret at the roll call by extending the lines in which they stood to be counted. The trick succeeded, although Dufour and Smit were caught on the run ten days later.

The inner courtyard at Colditz, used as a recreation and assembly area. The two Dutch escapers, Steinmetz and Larive are inset

Two days after Dufour and Smit, on Saturday, 15th August, it was the turn of Larive and Steinmetz. That day, in the park, an elaborate cover operation went into action. The two escapers lowered themselves into the well while a group milled round it apparently playing a ball game. At the same time, another prisoner, Lieutenant Dames, sat down under a tree near the barbed wire fence that ringed the park and ostentatiously began cutting a hole in it. When he started to crawl through, Dames, as planned, was detected at once. The Germans pounced on him, dragged him back and made him raise his hands in surrender. As he did so, Dames yelled out: 'Run! Run!' The call was taken up by other prisoners in the park and the Germans naturally assumed they were calling to prisoners who must have preceded Dames through the hole in the fence. Red-faced with fury, the Germans pushed the prisoners along the path out of the park and gave the alarm.

Meanwhile, Larive and Steinmetz had clambered down the iron rungs inside the well and into the water. There they stood, immersed chest high, holding over their heads the grey blanket they had brought with them as camouflage. If by any chance Germans search-

Diversionary tactics were often used by prisoners to conceal real escape attempts

ing the park discovered the cement slab, prised it open and looked down the well, all they would see in the dim depths was a grey mass that appeared to be still water. Or so the two Dutchmen hoped.

The camouflage was never put to the test. After two hours of shivering in dark discomfort, their arms aching intolerably as they held up the blanket, Larive and Steinmetz decided that the Germans were not going to discover the well. They crawled out of the water and perched on the iron ladder to wait for nightfall.

Larive and Steinmetz in the well. It proved an uncomfortable but successful refuge

It was during this wait that Larive eventually decided to risk lifting the concrete slab to allow air into their hideout and so avert the near certainty of suffocation.

At last, around 10pm, after seven hours in the well, Larive and Steinmetz saw the last of the light fade and the upraised edge of the slab grow indistinct against the sky. They crept to the top of the ladder, pushed up the slab and paused. There was no sound anywhere. No lights. Just pitch dark and stillness. Quickly, the two Dutchmen scrambled out, padded across the grass, climbed the barbed wire fence and made for the next obstacle, a brick wall about four metres high. Fortunately, there was a convenient tree close to it and Larive and Steinmetz were able to climb its branches and jump down the other side of the wall. In the darkness they were unable to judge the distance to the ground and the impact on landing jarred right through their bodies. As soon as they had recovered, they crept off, making for the railway station at Leipzig. The first train would arrive there at daybreak and Larive and Steinmetz planned to be on it.

Thanks to Larive's compass, the two of them reached the station in good time and Steinmetz, who spoke better German, bought two tickets. Larive, meanwhile, sauntered to the end of the platform and watched the distant figure of his companion standing by the ticket window. The proximity of Colditz, the constant chance of prisoners escaping and Larive's conviction that they must have been missed by now made it very likely that one or other of them would be challenged. If Steinmetz were caught buying the tickets, at least Larive could get away.

But nothing happened. Steinmetz walked along the platform to join Larive and when the train came, the two of them climbed in and settled quietly in their seats. The train soon moved off, rumbling on its way to Dresden, Ulm and Nuremberg. For Larive, it was a return journey of a sort: this was the rail route he had taken on his abortive escape from his previous prison camp. Now, as then, Larive's destination, and this time Steinmetz' too, was Singen, about two kilometres from the Swiss border. They got there at dusk on 17th August, two days after crawling out of the well in the grounds of Colditz.

The tree provides a convenient escape route

Everything had gone smoothly so far, but as they turned out of Singen station in the gathering dusk, Larive was suddenly overcome by apprehension. The strange, unaccountable feeling was soon justified. A kilometre from the frontier, the road entered a wood and just as the two men reached this point, a German guard appeared about 50 metres ahead. It was obvious from the way he quickened his pace that he had seen the two escapers; he was coming to check their papers, Larive thought. Suddenly it seemed to Larive that he was going through a horrible repeat performance of his previous escape, when a guard checking papers had caught him in almost the same place.

At that moment Larive spotted a path just ahead of them turning off the road back into the woods. The path would take them away from the frontier but it was that or be caught again. Larive and Steinmetz turned quickly down the path just as the guard yelled out 'Halt!' They ignored his shout and as they went haring along between the trees, Larive heard a bullet zing after them, missing them by an uncomfortably short distance. The two men plunged into the trees, expecting a second shot at any moment. None came and looking back, Larive saw that the guard had gone.

The German had probably left to raise the alarm. Larive and Steinmetz decided they had better go to ground and watch out to see what measures the Germans were taking in their search for them. They found a good observation post in a thick bush from which they could keep an eye on the road about 350 metres away.

They could also see the guardhouse and judging by the noise coming from inside it, the Germans there were preparing for a hunt.

It began to rain just as a group of guards emerged, climbed onto bicycles and moved along the road in line. Every 400 metres or so, Larive and Steinmetz saw one of them dismount and take up a guard position. Then suddenly, from somewhere behind them, they heard rifle shots and dogs barking. The fugitives crouched back in the bush, covered themselves with their grey blanket and waited. The noise came closer and closer. Larive was sure

Larive and Steinmetz approaching the frontier, notice a guard blocking their route to freedom

that a dog would come sniffing and growling through the shrubbery with an armed guard behind him. But slowly the sounds faded away into the distance until after 15 minutes they ceased altogether.

The Dutchmen remained huddled in the bush with the rain soaking them as it dripped down from the leaves, until ten o'clock at night. Only then did they feel safe enough to leave their hiding place. They crept through the trees until they reached the edge of the wood, then dropped down flat on their stomachs and crawled across the road.

A field of wheat lay a short distance ahead and Larive and Steinmetz moved warily through the crops, listening all the time for signs of danger. The village of Gottmadingen was quite close and the road from there ran straight into Switzerland. A few hundred metres along the road, they saw a signpost. They approached hopefully – could it be a Swiss frontier signpost? Moments later, they were pelting away from it as fast as they could go. It was a German customs post.

Had there been any sentries on duty there, they would have found the Dutchmen an easy catch. After nearly three days on the run with only a couple of bars of chocolate to sustain them and no sleep, Larive and Steinmetz were chilled through and bone weary. But fortunately, the customs post was not policed by sentries, and the Dutchmen stumbled on, sure that the Swiss frontier was only a few metres away. Then, about 15 minutes later, they spotted a cluster of houses. Swiss? Or German? They were leaning against the wall of a barn, exhausted and trying to decide the answer to that all important question, when the blinding beam of a torch came stabbing out of the darkness, and the sound of heavy boots squelching through the mud reached their ears. Larive and

The determined Dutchmen preparing to overpower the guard and make a dash for the border

Steinmetz were transfixed with fright. The torch played over them, right to left, top to toe, only a metre away.

'Who are you?' a gruff voice demanded. 'What are you doing here?'

Larive's heart sank. The man had spoken German. Larive was consumed with violent fury and tears sprang to his eyes. Not again, he thought in despair, and only about 50 metres from Switzerland. Then, anger was replaced by cold determination; if they could kick the man hard in the stomach, they could floor him for long enough to dash those 50 metres into Switzerland. Larive managed to whisper this thought to Steinmetz and the two men leaned back against the barn wall, each raising his right foot to brace himself for a mighty lunge. They were moments away from planting a powerful kick apiece when suddenly, they heard the man say: 'Sie sind in der Schweiz. Sie mussen mit mir kommen!'

The two Dutchmen sighed with marvellous relief. They felt like crying and laughing at the same time.

'You are in Switzerland,' the man had told them, speaking in German, which was one of the Swiss national languages. 'You'll have to come with me!'

CHAPTER 6

The Queen's Pearl Earring

*The boatman tried to
pull the muffler away, but Mary put
out a hand to stop him, and
that was her undoing.*

Lochleven Castle in Kinross-shire had all the qualifications of a perfect prison, and for the nobles who rebelled against their sovereign, Mary, Queen of Scots, in 1567, and made her their captive, it was an almost automatic choice. Place Mary there, the Scots lords reasoned, and she would be safely out of the way. Lochleven was remote and inaccessible, situated as it was on one of four islands in the middle of a lake or loch 20 kilometres wide. Also, Sir William Douglas, the laird who owned it, was no friend of the queen. As for escape, that was virtually impossible. There was no place to hide on the islands, since the great stone walls of the fortress-castle sheered straight up out of the water, and any attempt to get away by boat could easily be spotted from the five-storey main tower.

The isolation of Lochleven had another valuable purpose. It was far away from large towns and large crowds. There was nothing there but the Lomond hills frowning down upon the loch, and flat desolate surrounding shores holding only one small village. In sparsely habited country like this, Mary would be unable to use the most potent weapon she had against her rebel lords: her extraordinary charm and the publicity value of that charm.

At 25, Mary had already been for many years a celebrated beauty, and her romantic aura had often turned the heads of men and women alike, binding them to her in enduring

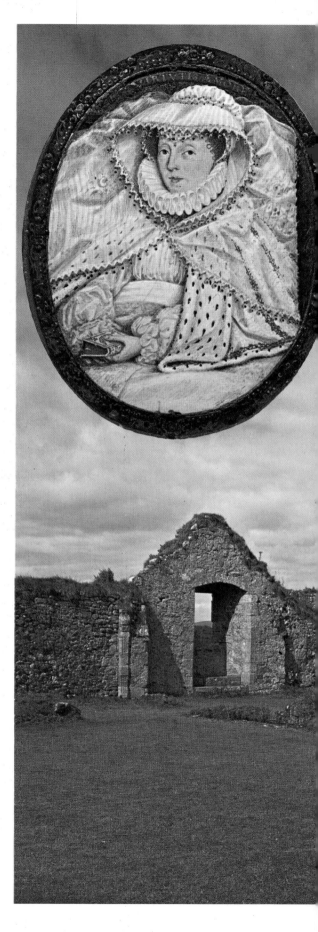

Inset: *Mary Queen of Scots painted by the famous Elizabethan miniaturist Nicholas Hilliard. Lochleven Castle today is little more than a ruin although still set in splendid isolation*

personal loyalty. Mary was, in fact, a remarkable example of the powerful attraction of womanly appeal combined with regal magic.

This power had already been displayed very effectively in Edinburgh in June 1567, when Mary was briefly confined in the Provost's house not long after being taken captive. The queen had appeared, distraught, at the window of her room in full view of a curious crowd down below. Her clothes were torn, her hair dishevelled, her face swollen with tears and she was crying out piteously that she had been betrayed and falsely accused. The people of Edinburgh, Mary begged, must not believe the dreadful lies they had heard about her: they were the work of traitors and renegades. The crowd, startled into sympathy at the sight of their distracted young queen, had soon begun to wonder about the truth of the allegations the nobles had made against her. Perhaps, after all, Mary was *not* guilty of conniving with the Earl of Bothwell to murder her husband, Lord Darnley. Perhaps, after all, the subsequent marriage of Mary and Bothwell was not, as they had been told, a wedding of accomplice and assassin. Soon, rumours started to spread round Edinburgh that in offering the queen's supposed 'crime' as reason for rebelling against her, the Scots lords were just using a shoddy excuse to cover their own thirst for power.

The nobles and in particular, Mary's dominant and ambitious half-brother, the Earl of Moray, were well aware of these whispers and knew how dangerous they were to their cause. A few more 'performances' like the one in Edinburgh, and there could well be a popular uprising in Mary's favour. Once she was restored to the throne of Scotland on a wave of popularity, that meant her husband, Bothwell, would be set up beside her as king. The idea of having such an odious upstart in such a powerful position was something Moray and his supporters could not entertain. They were determined it should never happen. Bothwell, they decided, was going to be hunted down and killed. Mary, in the meantime, was going to be isolated to stop her interfering with their plans.

Mary was removed from Edinburgh, hastily and in strict secrecy. She left on a dark night, accompanied by a strong escort, and was rushed deep into the countryside, to Kinross-shire. Finally, late one night, she arrived at the shores of Lochleven. There she was placed in a boat and rowed across the grey waters of the loch to the castle, where she was unceremoniously locked into a roughly furnished room.

The task of taking Mary to her bleak island prison had been easier than her captors had imagined. Mary herself had given little trouble. This was not surprising since the queen was in a state of shock and, in fact, spent the first fortnight of her imprisonment lying in a mournful stupor. For all its melodramatic appearance, her appeal to the crowd in Edinburgh had been no play-acting. Mary was then on the edge of nervous collapse. The cause was not simply the rebellion of her nobles, nor the flight of her adored new husband, Bothwell, who had managed to make his getaway just before Mary was taken captive. An important reason for Mary's

Mary is renowned for her beauty and often used it to win sympathy and support

enervated state was the sudden loss of the adulation she had been used to receiving all her life. Coarse-mouthed soldiers, obviously convinced of her guilt, had shouted insults at her along the road to Edinburgh. 'Burn her, she's not worthy to live!' some had yelled, while others chanted 'Kill her! Drown her!' Crowds in Edinburgh had shaken their fists at her, people had scorned and cursed her. In fact, Mary was made to feel that the whole country had turned against her.

No wonder that by the time she was hustled to confinement in Lochleven, Mary was sunk in deep depression. No wonder, either, that soon after her arrival she lost the baby she was expecting and became so ill that there seemed a definite chance she might die. Mary was still very weak and very depressed when Lord Lindsay, one of the rebel nobles, arrived at

Lochleven. Lord Lindsay, a thoroughly thug-like man, was well chosen for his task: he threatened Mary with violence or forcible removal to an even harsher jail, if she would not abdicate in favour of her baby son, James, the child of her short marriage to Lord Darnley. Mary signed, fearful that if she refused she might be killed. James, who later became King James I of England as well as James VI of Scotland, was crowned at Stirling on 29th July, 1567. He was then thirteen months old. The Earl of Moray was declared his Regent three weeks later, on 22nd August.

By this time, however, Mary had discovered that her personality still had the power to inspire sympathy and loyalty. The nobles who had shut her up in Lochleven had counted on the enmity of the Douglases to make her confinement secure, but they reckoned without the gallant and romantic spirits of two younger members of the family — George, a brother of Lochleven's owner, and Willy, an orphaned cousin known as 'the little Douglas'.

George, it appears, seriously entertained notions of marrying the queen, since the Earl of Bothwell had disappeared and was presumed to be dead. (Bothwell was, in fact, alive and had managed to escape across the North Sea to Norway.) Willy Douglas, utterly smitten by Mary's charm and beauty, took considerable risks for her by smuggling out the letters she wrote to Queen Elizabeth of England and Queen Catherine of France begging for their help in ending her imprisonment. Willy may or may not have realised it, but he placed himself in grave danger by carrying these letters, for in them, Mary asked for soldiers to be sent to lead a revolt in Scotland and so secure her release. Willy, in other words, was handling treason and it was fortunate for him that his activities were never discovered.

It was inevitable that, sooner or later, George and Willy Douglas would attempt to help Mary escape from Lochleven. Connivance and aid from the inside was, in any case, the only way such an escape could succeed. Mary had been made to realise this when, towards the end of April 1568, she had attempted to get away in a boat disguised as a laundress. The boatman became irritated when his passenger kept refusing to show her face and remained muffled up with only her eyes showing. He tried to pull the muffler away, but Mary put out a hand to stop him, and that was her undoing. Mary's smooth, white hand was very

Carnivals and elaborate pageants were common forms of entertainment in Elizabethan society

obviously not the sort that had ever scrubbed laundry in a tub and she soon found herself back in her room in the castle. At least, though, the boatman kept quiet about the abortive attempt and the Laird of Lochleven never got to hear of it.

Not long afterwards, when George Douglas began to plot another escape attempt for Mary, he took the wise precaution of bribing the boatman to cooperate with him. George's first idea was to hide the queen in a box and get the boatman to row it across the loch. The boatman, however, thought disguise a better method and George eventually agreed.

George crossed the loch to Lochleven village, where he busied himself arranging for horses to carry Mary away after the escape. Meanwhile, on the island, Willy Douglas took charge and arranged the timetable of events that would take place on the day of the breakout, 2nd May, 1568.

That day, Willy gave Lochleven castle a carnival atmosphere by organising a Mayday pageant. The castle was full of roisterous tomfoolery and Willy dressed up as an abbot making Mary follow him around for several hours. After emulating Willy's energetic antics, Mary was thoroughly tired, and in the afternoon she retired to her room to rest.

Mary's fatigue did, in fact, prove useful shortly afterwards. Willy was using pegs to make holes in the bottoms of all the boats by the shore, except one, when he was spotted by the Laird who happened to glance out of a window. The Laird was puzzled by this apparent lunacy which was, of course, designed to make the boats unfit to pursue Mary as she was rowed away across the lake in the single sound craft but after the ridiculous high jinks of the pageant, he was fortunately

Mary's escape was almost frustrated by the recognition of two local laundrywomen

shortly before supper, one of her maids brought a pearl earring to her. George Douglas, the maid told the queen, had recovered the earring from one of the local boatmen. What the maid was unwittingly telling Mary, because the earring had previously been chosen to signify it, was that everything was now prepared on shore.

This far, the furtive plans had been fairly easy to conceal. The feat which Willy Douglas performed later at the supper table was, however, extremely risky. If he were caught, the whole plot would be revealed. But luck was on Willy's side this time and while handing the Laird a glass of wine, he managed to escape detection as he eased the keys to the main gate out of the Laird's pocket. As the unsuspecting Laird downed his drink, Willy signalled to one of Mary's attendants.

Soon afterwards, wearing the rough hood and cloak of a local countrywoman, Mary walked across a courtyard full of servants and soldiers and reached the main gate. Willy unlocked the gate and after Mary and her companion had slipped safely through, he locked it again from the outside to hamper pursuit.

The boatman was waiting by the water with his boat and Mary stepped in, hiding herself under one of the seats. There were witnesses, though. Some laundrywomen recognised the queen and signalled their knowledge to Willy but he placed a finger on his lips and the women fell silent. They watched as the boatman pulled out across the loch and drew up on the opposite shore. There, George Douglas and Mary's own servant, John Beaton, were waiting with horses that Beaton had stolen from the Laird's own stables. The irony of this situation was not lost on Mary: she was escaping on her former captor's best mounts.

Mary and Willy Douglas sped away from Lochleven and by midnight, after several hours' hard riding and a sea crossing at Queensferry, they reached the palace at Niddry, near Winchborough, which was owned by her loyal supporters, the Seton family. As Mary approached this sanctuary, the local people greeted her with cheers. It was the first time in a year that Mary had heard the heartening sound of popular acclaim.

not too suspicious. In any case, Mary distracted his attention by pretending to faint from renewed fatigue and the Laird had to go and fetch a glass of wine for her.

There were other deliberate distractions, too. George Douglas returned to the castle and made a great show of saying farewell to his family: he was leaving Scotland, he announced, and was going to France for a while. The Laird was somewhat upset at the idea, but all the same, George departed and set out across the loch, ostensibly on his journey to foreign parts.

George had already set up the next stage of the escape, as became clear to Mary when

CHAPTER 7
Danish Exodus

The group of hospital workers grabbed the taxi driver, hauled him to the hospital refrigerator room and shoved him inside.

By the end of the Second World War, some six million Jews had been murdered at the hands of Adolf Hitler and the Nazi armies, and many thousands more had been hounded, starved and beaten in concentration camps. A similar number of Slavs, as well as countless political prisoners – German citizens among them – suffered the same fates. Hitler's hatred of Jews stemmed from the fact that together with socialists and communists he held them responsible for Germany's defeat in World War I.

As far as the Jews were concerned, Hitler's intention was to wipe the entire world free of Jews, but this plan was never completed, even in Nazi-occupied Europe. Among the fortunate ones who escaped the dreadful fate the Nazis planned for them were all but a few of the 7,000 Jews who lived in Denmark, the second country to be conquered by the Nazis after the war began in 1939. They were smuggled away at night, by sea, to the safety of neutral Sweden in an enterprise which concerned, even if only passively in sympathy, almost the entire population of Denmark.

The peaceable, freedom-loving Danes recoiled with loathing from the Nazi brutality to which they themselves were just as much subject as their Jewish compatriots. And at the risk of everything – their homes, their families, their freedom and their lives – they embarked, late in 1943, upon possibly the greatest mass escape Europe has ever known.

Although, in effect, Denmark was a conquered country during the Second World War, it was officially a Nazi 'protectorate' between 1940 and 1943, and its government and king, Christian X, retained some power over national affairs. Until 1943, this power was vigorously exercised to protect Danish Jews and fend off Nazi attempts to introduce special laws against them. The Danish attitude was made plain not simply in official government communications, which hinted at trouble if Denmark's Jews were touched; it was also paraded through the streets in spectacular fashion. No other word could describe what is reported to have happened when the Nazis demanded that Jews be forced to wear yellow distinguishing marks on their clothes. A great mass of non-Jewish Danes, King Christian included, turned

The Nazi presence in the streets of Copenhagen became more obvious as the war continued. The Danes lost no opportunity to stage protests against the Germans' treatment of the Jews

out onto the streets of Copenhagen, Denmark's capital, all of them wearing yellow armbands.

However, by the late summer of 1943, the Danes' power to stage protests like this was waning. The Nazis were getting impatient and, what was more, the war was going badly for them on the fighting fronts. This was particularly so in Italy, an ally of Nazi Germany, where the offshore island of Sicily had been invaded by British, American and other Allied

forces. With this, the Nazi empire in Europe was crucially threatened and the Nazis began to fear Allied attacks on Denmark's coast. The fear was reinforced when the Danes began to commit acts of sabotage against them.

All this combined to convince Adolf Hitler that Denmark must be brought under much stricter and more direct German control. As a result, the Danes suddenly found themselves afflicted with German military rule and martial law on 29th August, 1943, with their king imprisoned and his government dismantled. And this was how Denmark's Jews abruptly came to be in the front line of Nazi persecution.

The pattern of persecution was already a grimly familiar one. Germany before the war, and other occupied countries during the war, had all witnessed the raids on Jewish synagogues by the Gestapo (the Nazi secret police) the ransacking of records to pinpoint the names and addresses of Jewish families, the rounding up of Jewish communal leaders, the curfews and the plans to deport Jews to the concentration camps. The terrifying prospect of all this descended upon Danish Jews on 18th September, 1943, when the order for their deportation was signed in Berlin.

However, fortunately for them, not every German in Denmark was a Nazi Jew-baiter and

Jews being dragged out of their houses and thrown into trucks by German troops

among those who were not, was one man who was well placed to give valuable aid. G. F. Duckwitz, a maritime expert at the German legation in Copenhagen, was openly hostile to the anti-Jewish orders and he secretly informed two Danish politicians of the date fixed for the round-up of the Jews. The date was 1st October. Duckwitz passed on the information on 28th September, three days before that. The Danish politicians then informed the head of the Jewish community, the distinguished lawyer C. B. Henriques. The next day, 29th September, Danish Jews were gathering in their synagogues to celebrate the Jewish New Year when they were told the terrible news that Gestapo raids on their homes were imminent.

King Christian X of Denmark

On 1st October, the Gestapo squads went hammering and battering at the doors of Jewish homes only to discover, on kicking the doors in, that most were empty. All but a handful of Jews had fled to the safety offered by their non-Jewish friends and were, on that day, hiding in lofts, cellars, churches, coal holes or in hide-outs in the countryside. The tragic few the Gestapo caught owed their unenviable fate to their own naive faith in the power of King Christian to protect them. So revered was the courageous 73-year-old monarch and so great had been his influence, that these Jews were unable to believe they would come to any harm. When the Gestapo burst in through their front doors, they soon learned how dreadfully mistaken they had been. They were dragged out, pushed towards the trucks the Nazis had brought with them, thrown in and driven off to detention. Old men and women, the sick and infants in arms were all treated with the same disrespect and brutality as the fit and healthy.

For the Danes and for the Jews in hiding, the situation became quite clear – the Jews must be got out of the country before ruthless Nazi efficiency tracked them down.

No one person or group was responsible for the organisation that ensued, but overnight, a nationwide enterprise sprung up with everything needed for sheltering, and then for the mass exodus of over 6,500 Jewish men, women and children. Private citizens opened their homes as refuges; clergymen hid parties of Jews in parish halls and churches; and doctors and nurses hid more Jews in the wards

the short but perilous voyage across the water to neutral Sweden and safety.

Within days, groups of Jews were being smuggled into the harbours of Danish towns. There, on moonless nights, they scrambled up the gangways into ships moored by the dockside and then slipped across the decks and down into hiding in the holds.

Out in the country, on roads leading to the

Jews were smuggled out of Denmark by every possible means: by lorries, fishing smacks and rowing boats. German guards often turned a blind eye to suspicious 'cargoes'

or storerooms of hospitals. Danish policemen patrolled the streets on the lookout for the approach of Gestapo raiders. The coastal police, shipowners, port authorities, fishermen and dockyard workers gathered boats for transportation, and arranged pick-up points along the coast. Businessmen and industrialists provided money, fuel, food, paraffin and clothing – everything that was required for

coast, cars and van loads of Jews were driven with headlights dimmed to fishing hamlets or lonely coves and creeks. All along the coast, the darkened beaches came alive with small groups of people wading out towards an armada of fishing smacks, rowing boats and small sailing vessels. The fugitives clambered on board, soaked through and shaking with cold and trepidation, while lookouts posted on the roads and paths behind the beaches peered into the night, watching anxiously for fear a Nazi patrol might chance upon the furtive hive of activity.

Mothers hugged their infants and small children close to them, fearing that one cry or wail might give them away and bring disaster upon everyone involved. Old, bearded men, dressed in the traditional black coats and hats

of the very religious Jews, clung to their wives, children or grandchildren, trying to find some comfort and ease the fear that gripped them.

If all went well – and miraculously it did with gladdening regularity – the tight-packed boats were carefully rowed out, with silent dipping oars, until they were no longer visible from the shore. Night after night throughout October and November and into December 1943, the

escape went on until the Danish Jews taken across to Sweden numbered thousands. Everyone knew, of course, that the success rate owed much to certain sympathetic Germans who looked the other way at the right moment, or contravened orders by letting vehicles full of Jews pass through the road checks designed to catch them. At the same time, everyone also knew that certain traitorous Danes were

responsible for some of the failures and tragedies which the perilous venture involved.

It was never discovered who, if anyone, alerted the German patrol boat which suddenly roared up to a fishing vessel on 9th October, just as it was about to leave Taabaek harbour with its Jewish passengers. The patrol boat swooped in at speed, spraying bullets over the fishing boat's deck and crippling the engine.

The 20-year-old Danish engineering student, Claus Heilsen, who was in charge of the boat, tried to steer it back into the harbour, but the patrol boat went on firing round after round of ammunition and the young Dane dropped dead at the tiller, shot through the head.

More certain was the origin of the raid on 5th October which the Gestapo staged at a church in the coastal town of Gilleleje, where 163 Jews were sheltering while they waited for boats to take them to Sweden. The culprits were three Danish informers who came along with the Nazis to watch the results of their traitorous work. For hours, the Nazis battered at the thick, heavy doors of the church while inside, the Jews and their Danish helpers put up barricades and heaved against the doors to stop the Nazis entering. It was a hopeless battle of strength; the Gestapo finally man-aged to force a way in and arrested everyone in the church. The Danes were later released, but the Jews were all sent to Germany and the concentration camps.

On a happier occasion, Jews and a young Danish student, Peter Fhyn, were able to outsmart a potential betrayer when they discovered that the driver of a taxi taking them from a Copenhagen hospital to the harbour was a Danish Nazi. Peter stopped the taxi with some excuse, ran back into the hospital, and emerged a few minutes later with a group of hospital workers. They grabbed the taxi driver, hauled him to the hospital refrigerator room and shoved him inside to contemplate his treachery in a temperature several degrees below freezing point. Next day, festooned with frost, but still alive, the driver was taken out and revived. As soon as he opened his eyes and recovered his wits, he swore never again to collaborate with the Nazi authorities.

Peter's entire family – his parents, brother and a cousin – were involved in some way in the mass escape, all, of course, at their peril.

The Nazis battering down a church door in order to arrest the Jews sheltering inside

*Klinting, the female saboteur pretending to go mad
in order to get transferred to a hospital*

Mrs Fhyn, Peter's mother, spent hours sitting by the telephone, receiving messages that groups of fugitives were arriving or needed to be transported to the harbour. She was always careful not to use giveaway words like 'Jew' or 'saboteur' when talking over the telephone; the fugitives became 'a box of fruit', 'a crate of herrings' or 'cigarettes'.

Not all the 'fruit' and 'herrings' were Jews. There was, for instance, a solitary Negro who came to the Fhyns' apartment seeking help to get away and, of course, received it. Members of the Danish Resistance movement on the run also needed the escape route and often used it. One of them, a woman saboteur known as Klinting, was arrested by the Gestapo after she burned the plans of a new aircraft being produced for the Luftwaffe, the German air force. Klinting was flung into Vestre Faengsel prison, where she pretended she was seriously ill: she hoped to be transferred to a hospital, from where it would be easier to escape. But the Germans ignored her. Not to be outdone, Klinting then pretended to go mad. She screamed, bit and scratched her guards, wrecked her cell and attacked anyone who tried to come near her, until finally, the

Germans at Vestre Faengsel decided they had had enough. Klinting was removed to hospital, and the night before she was due to be transported to Germany, her friends in the Danish Resistance broke into her room and rescued her. At four o'clock the following afternoon, Klinting was on her way to Sweden with a party of Jews and other saboteurs.

While the refugees reached sanctuary in Sweden, the Fhyns, and numerous other Danish families who remained behind, were living in considerable and constant danger. Johannes Johannesen, the harbourmaster at Hellerup, Copenhagen, transported several groups of fugitives in coasters and always reckoned that at least 48 hours must pass after an escape before he could feel himself safe from the Gestapo.

After the war was over, a memorial was set up in Hellerup harbour, where Johannesen had put scores of Jews on board boats at enormous risk to himself and everyone who worked with him. It commemorates the great mass escape which, by the end of 1943, had transported all but an unfortunate 474 of Denmark's Jews across to the safety of Sweden. In the annals of organised mass escape, this has few, if any, equals. It is an outstanding example of how a love of freedom and an outraged sense of justice can prompt a whole nation to the selfless defence of a hounded minority.

75

CHAPTER 8
Destination Flushing

*There was more in the
paper Pluschow purchased from a
nearby news-stand. 'Extra late war edition –
Hunt for Escaped German!'
screamed the headlines.*

A few words overheard on the top of a London omnibus one morning in July, 1915, only a snatch of half-heard conversation between two businessmen, but enough to let Gunther Pluschow know he had found the solution to his problem: how, as an escaped prisoner of war hunted by the police, he could get out of England across the Channel.

'Dutch steamer . . . departure . . . Tilbury . . .' one of the businessmen was saying. Pluschow sat in the seat in front of them, straining his ears to hear more. Then, 'Destination . . . Flushing . . .' the man went on. 'Sailing . . . seven . . .'

Pluschow could not sit still a moment longer. Long before the bus arrived at its next stop, he was out of his seat, down the stairs and standing impatiently on the platform. As soon as the bus slowed down sufficiently, he leapt off and pelted towards the nearest station – Blackfriars. From there, he would make his way to Tilbury, where he fervently hoped he could get on board that Dutch steamer and at long last escape home to his native Germany.

People glared at Pluschow as he hurtled into Blackfriars station, slammed his fare down at the booking office, snatched up his ticket and dashed for the platform to await the train. The sight of what they took to be a dirty, malodorous docker – Pluschow's grimy disguise – naturally attracted disapproving attention when he went barging around like that. Had these Londoners known his true identity, their reactions would have been a lot stronger. As Pluschow well knew, the British harboured such hatred for Germans – their enemies in the First World War – that shopkeepers with

names that merely sounded German had had their windows smashed and themselves and their families beaten up and threatened.

It was an unnerving thought for Pluschow as he waited for the Tilbury train to arrive. He felt very tense and nervous. Relax, he told himself sternly. There was plenty of time; it would be foolish for him to risk making himself too conspicuous, and perhaps get caught again, on the very last lap of the long escape that had taken him halfway around the world.

It had begun thousands of kilometres from

Donington Hall set in the peaceful countryside around Derby. The house was rebuilt in 1793

London, in the German-controlled city of Kiaochow, in China. Soon after war had broken out in August 1914, Kiaochow had come under siege by strong British and Japanese forces. Gunther Pluschow, First Naval Flying Officer at Kiaochow, managed to get away by aircraft in November and crossed the Pacific to San Francisco. From there he travelled by train to New York, where he disguised himself as a Swiss locksmith and boarded an Italian steamer. Pluschow crossed the Atlantic safely but then, in January 1915, bad luck struck: the ship made an unscheduled stop at Gibraltar, where he was recognised and arrested by the British authorities. He was shipped to England and sent to the Donington Hall internment camp near Derby.

There, Pluschow schemed and waited for the right moment to escape. That moment arrived on the night of 4th July, 1915, and Pluschow scaled the barbed wire fence surrounding the prison camp, together with a naval officer called Trefftz. Both men were scratched all over and their clothes were ripped and torn, but both got clean away from Donington Hall and out into the quiet countryside around Derby. After a shave and a change into the clothes they had brought with them, the two Germans boarded a train then separated until they reached London.

The next evening, Pluschow arrived on the steps of St Paul's Cathedral where he and Trefftz had arranged to meet. He waited for an hour, but there was no sign of Trefftz. Another hour passed; still no sign. Pluschow decided to search Fleet Street and the Strand, hoping to meet Trefftz on the way. But he was nowhere to be found. When Pluschow got to the Strand, he learned why:

'Mr Trefftz has been recaptured,' huge, yellow posters announced. 'Mr Pluschow is still at large, but the police are on his track.'

There was more, far too much more, in the paper Pluschow purchased at a nearby newsstand. 'Extra Late War Edition – Hunt for Escaped German!' screamed the big headlines. To his dismay, Pluschow saw the paper had printed a short, but very detailed description of him: 'Height, 5ft 5½ins; weight, 135lbs; complexion, fair; hair, blond; eyes, blue; and tattoo marks: Chinese dragon on left arm.'

Pluschow's sleeve was drawn well down

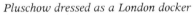
Pluschow dressed as a London docker

over that telltale tattoo, but the paper had also described what he was wearing. He must get rid of some of his clothes. Pluschow left his coat in the cloakroom at Blackfriars station, dropped his hat into the Thames at London Bridge and dumped his collar and tie further along the river. Then he set about the messy business of disguising himself. He rubbed oil, bootblack and coal dust into his hair until it was black and greasy. Next, he wallowed in a coal heap until his trousers, green shirt and blue sweater were smothered in black dust. At the end of his dirt-bath, the German looked exactly like a scruffy London docker who had probably not seen a washbasin for weeks.

The two businessmen who were travelling in the morning bus must have recoiled inwardly at the sight, and the smell, of Pluschow as he sat down in front of them. But they did the polite thing: ignored him and went on with their conversation. Pluschow sat half-listening to what they were saying; suddenly, he pricked up his ears. Unknown to them, the two businessmen were giving away wonderful news for an escaped POW – they revealed that a Dutch steamer sailed at seven o'clock each morning for the port of Flushing, having cast anchor close to Tilbury Docks the previous afternoon.

It took only a few minutes from the time Pluschow heard that welcome information until he was waiting impatiently for the Tilbury train on the station platform at Blackfriars. At last, the train appeared. Pluschow found a seat and settled down.

Now he was on his way, Pluschow relaxed a little. The smoke-blackened houses of east London passed before his eyes as the train clattered along the track. Here and there, between the houses, he caught a glimpse of the mean streets with their shabbily dressed inhabitants. This poverty-stricken part of London was so different from the clean, elegant, fashionable areas of Knightsbridge, Mayfair and Bloomsbury. Pluschow was re-lieved when the last depressing suburbs slipped past the train windows, to be re-placed by the serene and warm July green of the Essex countryside. He began to concentrate on what he was going to do.

Not long afterwards, Gunther Pluschow lay in the long grass by the riverside at Tilbury, pretending to doze in the sun. In reality, he was keeping a very sharp eye on what was happening along the waterway. As ship after ship went by, Pluschow anxiously scrutinised the names painted on their bows and the flags fluttering from their masts. Hours passed, and there was not a single Dutch vessel to be seen. Then, at around four in the afternoon, Pluschow saw the ship he had been waiting for. The Dutch steamer for Flushing came sailing majestically by and, with a sudden upsurge of emotion, Pluschow read the name on its bows: *Mecklenberg*. Mecklenberg-Schwerin was Pluschow's home province in

Germany. Surely, he thought, this must be a sign of good luck. It was natural and comforting to think so, but over the next few days, it seemed as if luck had deserted, not favoured, the escaping German prisoner.

After spotting the *Mecklenberg*, Pluschow hid among some wood and rubbish until midnight. Then, he crept out and looked around for a small boat that would enable him to row out to where the steamer lay at anchor. Almost immediately he noticed a dinghy moored just by some barges. He at once headed for it, scrambling over the rough ground as fast as he could go. Then, without warning, the ground gave way under him and with arms flailing wildly, he began to sink into a squelchy mass of swamp ground. Pluschow struggled with all his strength and was just able to fling himself far enough out of the swamp to grab a plank that fortuitously lay nearby. The swamp tried to suck him back, but he clung on and at last hauled himself free.

Exhausted by the effort and frightened at how close he had come to choking to death in the slime, he crawled back to his woodpile. At seven next morning, he watched dismally as the *Mecklenberg* sailed without him.

The next night, Pluschow tried again. He found another small dinghy moored by the river at a wharf which was watched over day and night by a sentry. When it got dark, Pluschow crept over the river embankment wall and crouched on the other side, listening to the heavy tramp of the sentry walking up and down. The little dinghy was rocking back and forth on the river only a few metres away. When the footsteps receded, Pluschow ran quickly down to the wharfside, snaked himself down into the boat feet first and huddled in some shadow at one end while the sentry, who was now returning, paced closer and closer. Any moment, thought Pluschow, heart thumping, the sentry might see him lurking below in the boat and yell a challenge. But the sentry saw nothing; he turned again and tramped away from the wharf.

Pluschow sighed with relief and was just blessing his luck when he saw the oars. They were shackled to the boat by great padlocks. For one dreadful moment, Pluschow thought his second bid to get to the *Mecklenberg* had met an untimely end, but he managed to saw through the padlocks with the Indian knife he carried, and then slipped the mooring ropes and began to row out towards the centre of the river. All seemed to be going well until, a few minutes later, the boat started taking in water. It poured in steadily, causing the boat to sink lower and lower until, with a terrible harsh grinding noise, the keel ploughed into the river bed and stuck fast.

Nothing would move it. Pluschow kicked at the gunwale, pushed with the boathook and shifted his body around in the hope that altering the weight inside the boat would make some difference, but nothing worked. Soaked through, utterly weary, despairing and stranded, Pluschow could have wept. Soon afterwards, the tide began to fall fast and before long, Pluschow found himself in the ludicrous position of sitting in a boatful of water on a mudbank laid bare by the receding waters. He sidled down onto the mudbank without the sentry seeing him, and wallowed around like an amphibian till he reached the embankment wall. Then he squelched back to his hiding place, still unseen, but caked in sticky mud and thoroughly dispirited.

Nevertheless, next night, he was determined to make another attempt. He combed the

Pluschow's second bid to reach the Mecklenberg *ending in disaster*

river bank until he found a small skiff bobbing in the water near some fishermen's huts. The group of fishermen sitting on a bench by the riverside, gossiping among themselves, failed to spot the swift-moving figure slipping down to the water only six metres away. Pluschow climbed into the skiff, loosened its moorings, gave a mighty push at the mooring post and glided off towards the middle of the river. Seconds later, he found himself being whirled round helplessly by the ebb tide. It took all his strength and nerve to regain control of the boat and steer it downstream, floating along with the current. Quite un-expectedly, a military pontoon bridge appeared in front of him with soldiers pacing along its length. One of the soldiers shouted out when he saw Pluschow and his boat, but the German ignored him and steered the boat quickly past the bridge and out of earshot – and gunshot.

Pluschow brought his tiny craft to a halt close to the shore and settled down to wait for

dawn to break. As the sun rose, lighting up the summer sky, the outlines of ships at anchor took shape before him. He could see *Mecklenberg*, back once more from Flushing, lying not far from him to starboard. Then, he realised something was very wrong. When he pushed off again, the tide felt far too strong. In so tiny a boat, he could never steer his way close enough to *Mecklenberg*'s side. With sinking heart, Pluschow realised what that meant – escape had eluded him again.

Glumly, he let the skiff drift downstream until he reached a crumbling old bridge. Tall clumps of coarse grass grew on the river bank at this point and here, Pluschow dragged his boat out of the water and lay down to wait for his next chance. Shortly afterwards, he had the infuriating experience of seeing *Mecklenberg* set sail and vanish down the waterway without him for the second time.

The day passed and Pluschow remained in hiding, hungry and thirsty, but determined to succeed next time. Darkness descended and he floated the boat out once more. As he was steering it upstream with the incoming tide, a wonderful and unexpected sight made his heart leap with joy. A Dutch steamer, *Princess Juliana*, lay straight ahead, moored to a buoy.

At midnight, when it was still and quiet on the river, Pluschow rowed silently out towards the steamship. The huge black hull of *Princess Juliana* towered above him as he pulled himself up onto the buoy, gave the skiff a hefty kick, which sent it spinning away, and then began to climb up the thick steel cable that led onto the steamer's deck. He reached deck level, poked his head over the rail to make sure that there was no-one about, then hauled himself up and pelted across the deck to the shelter of the windlass. All was quiet. No-one had noticed him. After resting for a moment, he

Above: *Gunther Pluschow wearing the Iron Cross*
Left: *Pluschow steering his boat past a bridge*

crept along the deck, slipping past two sentries who were engrossed in conversation. Still undetected, he reached a lifeboat, tore a hole in its cover with his hands and teeth and pulled himself down inside it.

The next moment, or so it seemed, Pluschow was abruptly awakened from a deep, exhausted sleep by the shrill blasts of the steamer's siren. Cautiously, he lifted the side of the lifeboat cover and peeped out. He only just managed to stop himself shouting out with excitement at what he saw: the *Princess Juliana* was steaming into Flushing! He was in Dutch territory, neutral free territory.

On 13th July, 1915, only nine days after climbing the barbed wire fence that surrounded Donington Hall, Gunther Pluschow arrived by train in Germany. His remarkable escape from England had already come to the attention of Kaiser Wilhelm II, the flamboyant ruler of Germany. Wilhelm loved a brave deed above everything else, and he was very impressed. The reward he gave Pluschow for his escape was the Iron Cross, First Class, the most coveted award for valour and enterprise his country could offer.

CHAPTER 9

Indian Impersonation

The first thing the guide wanted to know about the two fugitives was not their purpose or anything about their escape, but their initials.

Kalah had fainted. The British policeman's bullying tone and the near certainty of imminent discovery had proved too much for the Indian guide. One moment, Kalah was sitting on a blanket by the roadside, wide-eyed and flustered, his voice rising to hysterical pitch as he tried to answer the policeman's questions; the next moment, he had keeled over and lay slumped like a rag doll.

Elios Toschi, Kalah's Italian companion, was appalled and astounded. He was disguised as a Pathan from northern India but he got ready to run for it in case the policeman showed signs of guessing his true identity. The truth – that Toschi was no Pathan, but an escaped prisoner of the Second World War – seemed likely to dawn on the policeman at any moment. He was thoroughly suspicious and was firing a long, searching stream of questions at the two men with machine gun rapidity. No wonder Kalah had been so frightened. Toschi, however, could not afford to let himself be so overcome: he had to keep his nerve or all would be lost. With unflinching courage, he squatted by the roadside and let the barrage of questions wash over him.

What was his name? Where had he come from? Where was he going? Had he seen any Italians? Or anyone else suspicious?

The torrent of questions poured on, then stopped. The policeman began to demand answers – at once, this minute! Toschi knew his only hope was to play the part of the dimwit Pathan. He gazed blankly at the policeman, shrugged and in a voice denoting apathetic indifference said: 'Kayah patan?' – 'Who knows?'

Elios Toschi had been a prisoner of war in British India for two years, since June 1941, long enough to know that there was nothing more deflating than this phrase, which Indians often used to avoid giving an explanation. They just let their opponents run out of questions or steam or both, and then pricked the balloon of their argument with those two enigmatic words.

This was precisely the effect on the British policeman. Suspicion was replaced first by puzzlement, then by contempt. These two Indians, the policeman had clearly decided, were nothing but a couple of idiots. To Toschi's overwhelming, but carefully concealed relief, the policeman abruptly turned and stalked off down the road, his hobnailed boots ringing out on the asphalt.

The British policeman questioning Kalah and Toschi as they crouch by the roadside. Inset: *Toschi disguised as a Pathan Indian*

Toschi silently blessed all the saints in his native Italy at the hair's-breadth escape from recapture he had just had. It would not have been a new experience to be caught on the run, he reflected ruefully. This bid, in February 1943, to reach neutral territory in the tiny Portuguese island enclave of Diu was no less than his ninth attempt to escape from captivity.

Captivity had overtaken Elios Toschi, a submariner in the Italian Navy, early on 30th September, 1940, barely four months after Italy had entered the Second World War as an ally of Nazi Germany. The previous night, in the Mediterranean near Alexandria, Toschi's submarine *Gondar* was attacked with depth charges by a force of British destroyers. The damage *Gondar* sustained proved serious enough for the crew to have no alternative but to surface the submarine, even though surfacing in a sea full of British ships meant inevitable capture. Not long after emerging into the Mediterranean morning with oil, wreckage and other survivors floating around him, Elios Toschi was glumly climbing a rope ladder onto the deck of the British destroyer *Stuart*, where he gave himself up. He felt utterly dejected. For him, the War had ended in capture and imprisonment on what was only his second venture against the enemy.

Survivors of the Italian submarine Gondar *are rescued by British destroyers*

The energy Toschi had geared up for war was, however, soon concentrated on the business of escape. In his first attempt, he tried to tunnel out of prison camp at Geneifa near the Suez Canal. But that venture was frustrated when his British captors decided to send all the prisoners there to India. Toschi was plunged into despair. India was another world, totally alien, totally unknown and thousands of kilometres from his Italian homeland. This initial melancholy at the prospect of imprisonment in India wore off during the eighteen-day sea voyage to Bombay, where Toschi and the other Italian prisoners were due to arrive late in October 1940. During the voyage, Toschi and a fellow prisoner, Camillo Milesi, prepared an escape hatch in one of the toilets. They planned to climb through it, onto the deck and then onto the quayside when their prison ship docked at night. The escape never took place. The British unexpectedly decided to disembark their prisoners in the full blaze of the Indian afternoon.

Neither Toschi nor Milesi was deterred. Soon after the train taking them to prison camps south of Bombay pulled out of the station, Milesi first, then Toschi, jumped from their compartment window onto the track. They planned to hire a car and make for the Portuguese enclave of Goa, about 420 kilometres down the coast from Bombay. The two Italians got tantalisingly close to freedom. They did in fact reach the Goan border, but an official at the Customs Post became suspicious and, to their chagrin and fury, their true identity was revealed. Soon afterwards, they were taken under armed guard to Ahmadnagar camp, high up in the Deccan mountains above the western coast of India.

Just over two years, several prison camp transfers and four more failed attempts later, Elios Toschi knew a great deal about the means, the supplies and the preparations needed for successful escape from captivity in British India. Through diligent, clandestine study – such knowledge was forbidden by the British – Toschi also learned a great deal about the geography, climate and inhabitants of the vast Indian subcontinent, and about the timetables that regulated the movements of trains in its huge railway network.

Toschi and Milesi attempting to escape from the train taking them to prison camp near Bombay

In addition, Toschi acquired hard-earned knowledge of how *not* to escape from confinement. Tunnelling, for instance, was hopeless: no less than three tunnel ventures in which Toschi was involved were foiled. It was also futile to rely on prison camp routine to aid an escape: Toschi's seventh attempt to get away ended in failure when, for the first time in months, a camp gate normally left open was closed; Toschi, who had been hiding in a nearby hut, was confronted with an impenetrable rank of padlocked iron bars.

Escape number eight taught Toschi how vital it was to have either reliable Indian helpers on the outside or no helpers at all. This became dismally clear when Toschi and two other Italians, who escaped from a prison camp 5,000 metres up in the mountains of northern India, were trapped in a forest clearing by military police alerted by an Indian informer. That was in May 1942, when the Italians, who were making for neutral territory in Tibet, had been on the run among the freezing snows, perilous passes and isolated villages of the Himalayas for two months.

With all this experience behind him, Toschi planned his ninth escape with great care and took his time about it. For some while, he contemplated a solo escape from his camp, near Yol village, deep in the mountain slopes of the Himalayas. But eventually, after encountering reluctance and ridicule from other prisoners, he found a reliable companion, a second lieutenant called Anastasio. Toschi's planned destination, the Portuguese island enclave of Diu, was 2,500 kilometres away to the west, an enormous, impossible distance he was told and he was assured, too, that his disguise, as a Pathan, would never succeed. No European had yet successfully disguised himself as an Indian; no colouring produced from burnt cork, burnt sugar, permanganate, vegetable dye or even sunbathing had ever managed to reproduce the distinctive greyish dark brown of the true Indian's skin.

Toschi, nevertheless, was convinced he had chosen his disguise well. Fair skinned, taller and brawnier than many Indians, Pathans were very European in their general appearance. As for Toschi's distant destination, he was by now an expert on Indian railways and their routes and knew that if he and Anastasio could reach the plains below Yol and the prison camp, trains would provide transport all the way to the west coast.

Toschi's most important asset for this ninth escape was an absolutely loyal and trustworthy Indian friend, a thin, bony peasant farmer called Kalah, who had already aided him in his unsuccessful attempt to cross the Himalayas into Tibet.

Although no Italian at Yol, apart from Anastasio, was convinced that Toschi had at last devised the formula for a successful escape, all were willing to cover up for them and give them the best possible chance of getting away from the camp.

On a February evening in 1943, Toschi and Anastasio lay hidden under a pile of timber in a hut near the edge of the camp, listening for the signal that would tell them their absence had not been detected. The signal was the tramp of marching feet as the prisoners were dismissed and returned to their quarters after roll call. All went well. From the droning tone of the British guards in charge of roll call, they were obviously unaware that two prisoners were missing, and when orders to dismiss were followed by their fellow prisoners marching away as usual, Toschi and Anastasio knew that this far, they had succeeded.

A short while later, through the window of the hut, Toschi spotted his friend Faggioni taking a leisurely stroll, as previously arranged, close to the barbed wire. It was getting dark, and Toschi could see stars blinking in the blue Himalayan sky. As he watched, Faggioni pulled a large handkerchief from his pocket and loudly blew his nose in it. Toschi and Anastasio waited, hearts thumping. Faggioni blew his nose again. That meant the two British sentries had their backs turned.

Toschi and Anastasio tiptoed from the hut, slipped into the shadow of another hut further along the camp boundary, then dropped flat on the ground and wriggled towards the outer wire that ringed the camp. The two men squirmed under the fence and out into the darkness that lay beyond.

They reached Kalah's house at about midnight. The Indian was delighted to see them, though rather bewildered, since after eight failures, he had never dreamed that Toschi would be mad enough to try to escape again. However, Kalah unhesitatingly offered the Italians his house to hide in for the night, and next morning sent for a guide to accompany them on their forthcoming journey.

When the guide arrived, Toschi and Anastasio were nonplussed to find that the first thing he wanted to know was not their purpose, or anything about their escape, but their initials. Mystified, the two Italians watched as the guide thumbed through a large book he had brought with him. Kalah, seeing their puzzlement, explained: 'He is an astrologer. He is consulting our Hindu gods about what is to happen.'

To the Italians' relief, the gods seemed to decide in their favour. After several minutes of leafing through the book, consulting this page and that and generally giving the impression that he was deep in highly complex calculations, the guide finally closed it in triumph and announced: 'You will reach your destination.'

Two days later, when Toschi was sitting by the roadside being grilled by the British policeman, with the unconscious form of Kalah slumped beside him, it crossed the Italian's mind that Hindu astrology was not a very trustworthy science. Unforeseen fate seemed about to contradict the assurance of success promised by the gods, for the policeman's untimely appearance was the third stroke of ill-luck to occur within a few hours.

The two Italians, with Kalah and the astrologer-guide, had safely negotiated the steep, wooded paths and small streams that lay between Kalah's house and the asphalt road that

Toschi and Anastasio squirming under the fence and into the darkness beyond

led to Sarna, where the escapers planned to get on a train. They had about 160 kilometres of road to cover, but after only 30 kilometres, things began to go wrong. First, the astrologer-guide disappeared with money Anastasio gave him to buy a pair of sandals in a nearby village. Then, Anastasio went off on his own to find the house of an Indian friend of his where they could shelter for the night, but failed to return at the arranged time. The policeman seemed, in these melancholy circumstances, to be the last straw. At any moment, Toschi expected to be revealed for what he was, arrested on the spot and marched off for the ninth frustrating time back to prison camp.

Miraculously, this did not happen. The policeman failed to penetrate Toschi's disguise and marched off down the road. Toschi's faith in astrological predictions was restored immediately. Almost straight away, the gratifying idea that some unseen power was smiling, not frowning, on his efforts was reinforced. A muffled voice came from nearby trees, calling Toschi's name. The foliage parted and there was Anastasio, back at last. Toschi and Kalah – now completely recovered from his faint – leapt up and waved their arms delightedly to welcome him.

Anastasio had reappeared at just the right time. It was well past daybreak by now and in India, the daylight does not creep up on the sky, but floods it with brightness in a short space of time. A hiding place where they could pass the daylight hours was urgently needed and fortunately, Anastasio's Indian friend had told him of one: a broken down, long deserted and neglected mill, close to a nearby river.

Toschi slept most of the day away inside the mill, but awoke to find he was still tired. The tension of the encounter with the policeman, the intense, scorching heat of India in a season in which the sun shines unceasingly day after day, the hunger after several days without proper food – all these had combined to enervate the Italian and make the next night's march something of an ordeal. In addition, Toschi and his companions were suffering from tormenting thirst and had resorted to sticking out their tongues in the night air to try to get some moisture from it.

Nevertheless, despite the hardships and

fatigue, the three men tramped on for several more nights, passing through thick forests and plunging ravines to follow the road as it wound over the hilly terrain. Then, at long last, they heard the sharp whistle and rumbling on iron rails that denoted a train. They had reached the railway.

At dawn just over 24 hours later, after covering the last few kilometres to Sarna station, Toschi stood waiting for the train on the platform while Anastasio, who spoke Urdu

*The two Italians travelling to freedom. Toschi's
disguise surprises even himself*

sufficiently well, bought tickets. The Italians
felt triumphant. Diu, now about 2,250 kilometres away, could be reached entirely by
train. They did, however, have one regret.
Kalah had vanished the previous evening. He
had said he was going to buy some tobacco, but
he had never returned. Perhaps, Toschi reflected, Kalah knew the greatest peril of the
escape was now over and he could safely return
home.

Shortly afterwards, Toschi and Anastasio
were sitting in a third class compartment,
thinking the hard, wooden benches were
luxury after the rough living of the last few
days. Suddenly, Toschi caught sight of himself
in the train window. He was startled. No wonder the British policeman had never guessed he
was an Italian naval officer on the run. His face
was grey and ingrained with dirt, his beard

93

black, thick and tangled, and his turban smeared and filthy. So much the better, Toschi thought. The more he looked like a Pathan, the less likely it was that he would be spotted during the many changes of train that would have to be made on crowded stations during the next few days.

Day after day, Toschi and an equally scruffy Anastasio sat in trains which slowly crawled across the vast breadth of India. They passed through cultivated fields, arid deserts, thick forests and sunburned plains – the whole varied panorama of the great subcontinent – until at last, an unaccustomed smell, the fresh, salt tang of the sea, told them they were approaching the west coast. Toschi peered out of the train window and saw in the distance the shimmering haze reflected from the surface of the ocean. As the train moved on towards the coast, the shimmer grew brighter and spread further along the horizon.

Greatly excited, for they were now only about 12 kilometres from Diu and freedom, Toschi and Anastasio left the train one station

before the end of the line. It was getting dark as they descended onto the platform at Una and took the road that would lead them down to the shore opposite the island of Diu. They reached the darkened beach a few hours later. Peering across the black water, the two Italians could just pick out the low-lying mass of the island, with lights blinking here and there along its length. Diu, once an 'impossible' 2,500 kilometres away was now only 450 metres distant.

Next morning, Toschi and Anastasio covered those last few metres of their journey on the dawn ferry. The ferry chugged across from British India on the mainland, where they were fugitives on the run, and tied up minutes later at the landing stage on Diu, where they were at long last free men on neutral territory.

The Italians leapt onto the landing stage with feelings that were not far from ecstasy. They started running towards the beach and a gateway that led to the main town beyond, when suddenly, a fierce yell sounded out behind them. The two men froze, terrified. It flashed across Toschi's mind that now, at the very last moment, after all they had suffered, some British official had caught up with them.

Hearts thumping, they turned to see the ferryboat man glowering at them. He was holding out his hand and mouthing fierce phrases which neither Toschi nor Anastasio could understand. For a moment, the two Italians were nonplussed. Then, as they stared at the Indian's outstretched palm, the truth dawned on them. In their elation and excitement, they had forgotten to pay him for the journey that had taken them to freedom.

Freedom within their grasp, the two Italians cannot understand the Indian's anger

CHAPTER 10

Death Sentence

*Suddenly, a dozen
bullets came whistling through the
canvas of the tent in which Thomas lay,
closely guarded by two of
the Ruffians.*

He was trapped. Thomas Tibbles knew there could be no escape from the two men who were blocking the doorway of his hotel room. There they stood, brandishing their guns, leering at him. Thomas was lying on the bed, weary and aching from his recent journey; one move to get to the window or to try to push past into the corridor and that would be that: the two men would shoot him down without a moment's thought. Nor would they have any regrets afterwards. Men like them were not called 'Border Ruffians' for nothing. They were a lawless, unscrupulous lot, without conscience or mercy. Their leader, 'Colonel' William Titus, was one of the most feared and hated thugs in the whole of the central United States. Titus was particularly feared by the Negro slaves whom he kidnapped from the plantations where they worked and sold to new masters as cruel as he was himself. And he was particularly hated by the abolitionists, the people who for religious or humanitarian or other reasons, abhorred slavery.

Thomas Tibbles, though only 18 years old, was an ardent fighter against slavery and now, in the small Mid-West town of Lecompton on 10th September, 1856, he had been trapped by two of Titus's men, men to whom the word 'abolitionist' was the most hated in the dictionary. The two Ruffians ordered young Thomas to his feet. Then, one of them grabbed him by the shoulder and pushed him through the door of the room. They were going to the Ruffians' camp outside town.

It was obvious that people in the street knew what was happening, for as the Ruffians marched along with Thomas they looked away or scurried into shops, around corners or anywhere else where they could get quickly

out of sight. Thomas did not blame them. They were afraid and wanted to avoid trouble. Townspeople living in small communities in the west of the United States, where there was still a lot of lawlessness and violence in the middle of the 19th century, knew only too well what would happen if thugs like the Border Ruffians got upset or bothered. They were quite capable of shooting up a whole town or setting it on fire and beating or kidnapping everyone they could lay their hands on.

Not everyone, and certainly no-one out in Lecompton on that afternoon in 1856, pos-

sessed the brand of zealot's courage that made Thomas Tibbles risk his life for the cause he so fervently believed in. Thomas had become well known as a fearless, outspoken campaigner against slavery, travelling from one small town to the next to give passionate speeches condemning what he thought was a heinous evil. He raged against plantation owners who worked their slaves until they dropped in the fields, or beat them up or otherwise ill-treated them. In common with other abolitionists he challenged vigorously that anyone had the right to acquire riches the way slave owners did – by using negroes as cheap labour in their cotton and sugar-cane fields. Slavery, Tibbles never ceased to preach, was a dreadful act of inhumanity and wickedness and had to be abolished.

Border Ruffians were well known for taking completely unscrupulous violent action

Unusually, for a white person, Thomas Tibbles knew what he was talking about from personal experience, for at the age of eleven, he had been taken away from his mother and family and forced to labour for a cotton farmer in Iowa. The man had been no better than a slave driver; he forced Thomas to work in the fields from four in the morning until nearly midnight. Then, after a barely edible and always insufficient meal, Thomas was allowed only a few hours sleep on rough straw in a barn, before he was driven back to the fields to labour through another 18-hour day. After a year, he ran away and fortunately, was able to remain free.

That year in bondage turned Thomas into a crusader against slavery, but he never doubted that he was taking up a highly dangerous occupation. All the more so for him, because he was not afraid to condemn the supporters of slavery by name, and to do so in places where his condemnation could reach their ears.

In Kansas the problems of whether the territory should be slave-holding or free took an acute form when the decision was left to the residents of the state. Pro-slavery posters were common and soon guerrilla warfare raged across the land

As he toured the Mid-West during the summer of 1856, speaking out against slavery and slave owners and dealers to anyone who would listen, the man Thomas condemned most frequently was Colonel William Titus. Not surprisingly, on hearing this, Titus decided that Thomas was one abolitionist who must definitely be silenced. His chance came when news reached him that Thomas was in Lecompton; he wasted no time in sending two of his Ruffians to kidnap him.

Titus was ready and waiting for Thomas as soon as the two Ruffians marched him into camp. There was to be a trial next morning, Titus told the boy, and the charge was 'being an abolitionist and preaching abolitionism in public'. Thomas knew in that moment what the verdict was going to be and he wondered why Titus should even bother with a trial,

since he was so intent on his death. But William Titus was one of those people who, while they have no real respect for the law, nevertheless feel compelled to observe forms of law such as a court trial. It was this strange compulsion that ultimately created enough delay to save Thomas Tibbles' life.

The trial opened next morning at Lecompton courthouse. Thomas took the opportunity to speak out against slavery once again and possibly with more than his customary fire and spirit, since he was convinced it would be the last time he would ever be able to do so. He noted with disgust and despair that the

Tibbles and other anti-slavers took every opportunity to speak out against slavery

jury, specially gathered by Titus to ensure the verdict he wanted, included men like the local sheriff and a United States marshal. Such men should have been concerning themselves with enforcing the law rather than conniving with thugs like the Border Ruffians. The 'guilty' verdict was, of course, duly arrived at. So was the equally predictable sentence of death. Thomas Tibbles, the judge pronounced, would die by hanging the next morning, 12th September.

After the trial, Thomas was marched back to the Border Ruffians' camp, pushed into a tent and made to lie face down on the ground, with two armed men watching over him. Later, towards evening, an officer came into the tent to give instructions to the guards. Thomas, still lying on the ground, heard with some excitement that there were armed abolitionist soldiers in the Lecompton area. However, the Ruffians' instructions about what to do if the camp was attacked, or if Thomas tried to escape, were very clear: they were simply to shoot him at once.

The hours passed. The guards dozed from time to time, then woke with a start to peer at their prisoner. Thomas slept fitfully. It was very quiet outside. Then, suddenly, the young prisoner jerked awake. The pale light of dawn was seeping in under the tent and he could hear the sound of shooting nearby. Cries and yells mingled with the gunfire. The abolitionist troops were attacking the camp and a fierce fight was in progress.

Suddenly, a dozen bullets came whistling through the canvas of the tent in which Thomas lay; he watched as they ripped out through the other side of the tent. Then, a shadow fell across him. One of the guards was looming over him, his musket at his shoulder, ready to fire. The guard's finger was just curling round the trigger to shoot Thomas at point blank range when the boy sprang up, threw himself at the musket and jerked the barrel out of the way. The musket went off and a bullet ripped through the sleeve of Thomas's shirt. Almost at the same moment,

Violent skirmishes like this were a common prelude to the American Civil War

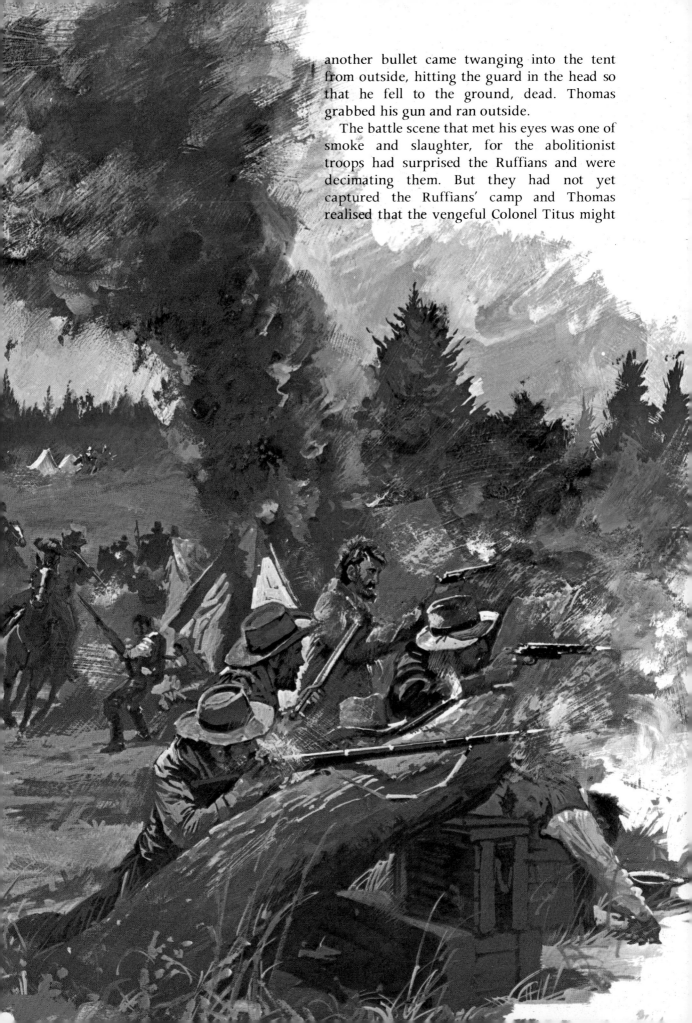

another bullet came twanging into the tent from outside, hitting the guard in the head so that he fell to the ground, dead. Thomas grabbed his gun and ran outside.

The battle scene that met his eyes was one of smoke and slaughter, for the abolitionist troops had surprised the Ruffians and were decimating them. But they had not yet captured the Ruffians' camp and Thomas realised that the vengeful Colonel Titus might still have time to carry out the execution of his hated young enemy. Thomas crouched down and ran across the camp with cross-fire zinging all around him. He reached the officers' quarters and ran into one of the bedrooms where, to his surprise, he found Colonel Titus propped up against one wall. Titus's right shoulder was heavily bandaged but still seemed to be bleeding badly and he was obviously in a great deal of pain.

Thomas stood there. This was a very different Colonel Titus from the vicious, swaggering bully who had made him stand trial the previous day. As soon as Titus saw Thomas, he began to cringe and cry out for mercy. His hand trembled violently as he put it up to defend himself against the musket ball he was sure Thomas was going to shoot into him. He would do anything, he told Thomas — surrender the camp, give himself up to the

Like many swaggering bullies, Colonel Titus was nothing but a craven coward

abolitionists, anything – so long as Thomas would let him live.

It was a pitiful and contemptible sight; like so many bigoted bullies, Colonel William Titus was a coward at heart. But Thomas showed Titus the mercy for which he so ignominiously pleaded and shortly afterwards, the Colonel and his surviving Ruffians gave

Border Ruffians were lawless, ruthless bands of men who killed and plundered without mercy

themselves up and the white flag of surrender fluttered over the camp.

Some years later, Ruffians and abolitionists, including Thomas Tibbles, faced each other on opposite sides of the American Civil War, which began in 1861. This war, fought between the southern states, who wanted to keep slavery, and the northern states, who wanted to abolish it, ended in 1865 with victory for the North and triumph for the abolitionist cause. Thomas Tibbles, at 25 already a veteran crusader for the oppressed, then turned his attention to championing another unfortunate and misused people – the American Indians.

However, the few hours he spent under sentence of death in the Ruffians' Camp outside Lecompton in 1856 remained an undimmed and vivid memory for the rest of his life. It was, Thomas wrote, 'the most nerve-wracking escape of my career'. That was an understatement. When Colonel Titus surrendered to the abolitionists who had invaded his camp, the time was 7 o'clock in the morning. Only one hour later, Thomas Tibbles was due to have ended his young life on the gallows.

CHAPTER 11

Escape from Germany

*It was almost midnight,
and the two escapers sat waiting
tensely until the right moment arrived – when
the train next slowed down.*

The German in soldier's uniform was approaching with a scythe in his hand, looking as if he meant to use it. Evans and Buckley were too exhausted and too footsore to try to run away. In any case, there was that other German only about 45 metres off with a gun. Even if they had a mind to bolt in the gathering dusk of that June evening in 1917, the two English officers could never have run far enough fast enough to get out of the gun's range. And they hadn't endured the hardships in getting this close to the Swiss frontier – and to freedom – just to get shot in the back.

The man with the scythe was scrutinising them, his small, unintelligent eyes scanning what looked to him like two very scruffy tramps dressed in filthy, frayed clothes, pale and gaunt from lack of proper food and water, and with several days' growth of beard bristling on their chins. These two strangers could, possibly, be tourists on a walking holiday, but even the most devout open-air enthusiast was unlikely to let himself get into their dilapidated state. In any case, the man with the scythe reflected, when these two had passed him as he was cutting the grass by the roadside, he had spoken to them and they had failed to answer. It was all very odd.

Evans and Buckley boldly confronting the suspicious German soldier

The fact was, that although Evans and Buckley spoke German well, they had not understood the southern German dialect the man had used. What he had said was quite incomprehensible to them, so they had just walked on past. It proved a small, but potentially perilous mistake. That became clear very quickly when the man called out: 'Alt! Alt!' and came running down the road after them, scythe still in hand.

Only nerve and effrontery were going to save them now, and Buckley used both. As the German came close, suspicion showing all over his face, Buckley let out a stream of angry swear words in a voice trembling with fear, but sounding like indignation.

What did the German mean by calling 'Alt!' to them in that insulting fashion? Who did he think he was? 'Really,' Buckley loudly confided to the equally tense Evans, 'southern Germans are such moronic oafs!' Evans agreed: 'The man is nothing but a South German pig-dog!'

The subject of these insults listened, eyes growing wider with amazement as the seconds passed. After a few moments, he was gawping at Evans and Buckley, wondering at his own daring in challenging them at all. Intimidated by their obvious outrage, the German turned without a word, walked back to the roadside and started scything the grass again. The two Englishmen then noticed with relief that the man with the gun had already lost interest in them and was gazing out over the fields.

Acting Captain A. J. Evans and Lieutenant S. E. Buckley, both of the Royal Flying Corps, both prisoners of the First World War on the run in hostile Germany, turned and walked off, loudly assuring each other that they had never before been so insulted. But even as they simulated fury they were trembling with relief, for they knew that with less luck, they could easily have ended up spending the night in some local jail, waiting for prison camp guards to come and take them back to captivity.

The value of luck in an escape was something Evans had learned not only from his own experiences but from those of the other inmates at the German prisoner-of-war camp, Fort IX, where he had been sent in November 1916. You needed luck to lie low in woods or fields all day without being discovered. You needed luck to walk unscathed through villages where everyone was on the lookout for escaped prisoners. You needed luck to speak to Germans in their own language, to ask directions and pass the time of day, without their detecting a trace of English accent.

It was when your luck deserted you that you ended up in a place like Fort IX. This daunting, dismal fortified mound, some 320 metres long and 20 metres high, was a camp for inveterate escapers: the Colditz Castle of the First World War. The site was perfect for its purpose, set as it was 11 kilometres from Ingolstadt in Bavaria, in flat, featureless terrain where escaping prisoners could easily be seen by guards on the battlements. In addition, Fort IX was equipped with two batteries of guns and ringed by a moat up to two metres deep.

A. J. Evans had qualified for Ingolstadt when he escaped from his previous prison camp,

Clausthal in the Harz Mountains: he had been sent there in July 1916, after his spotter aircraft crash-landed behind the German lines during the battle of the Somme. One dark night about two months later, Evans had cut through the wire surrounding Clausthal with nail pincers, then hurtled across a lighted strip round the camp perimeter and off into the darkness beyond. He struck northwards by train and on foot for the Dutch-German border and actually got to within 20 metres of freedom when an alert frontier guard grabbed him.

A few days afterwards Evans was back inside Clausthal. Liberty had been so tantalisingly close to him that it required little of the Germans' imagination to realise how much he must be itching to try again. So, before he could do so, the Germans shovelled him off to the closer confines of Fort IX.

Once through the heavy iron and barbed wire gates of his new prison, Evans found himself in an environment very different from Clausthal. For Ingolstadt was a place where inmates talked, dreamed and planned little else but escape. Escape had been discussed at Clausthal, and several prisoners apart from Evans had attempted to get away. However, many men there had seemed content to regard imprisonment as a welcome rest from the horrors of the battlefield. Prisoners at Ingolstadt were all familiar with the massacre, fear and despair on the war front, but this had no effect on their plans to abscond. At Ingolstadt, someone was always at some stage of an escape scheme – drawing maps, devising disguises, sharpening table knives to cut through bars, making keys, hoarding food.

Escape attempts were made by hiding in laundry baskets or dustbins full of rubbish. Some men planned to dress as German officers and bluff their way past the three sets of iron gates and the guardhouse that secured the camp. One prisoner even painted his face green and made a bid to swim the moat in daylight, hoping the sentry would mistake him for a water lily. More than once, ingenious courage like this earned prisoners a few days or hours of freedom before they were caught. Sadly, failure was more common than success and prisoners were regularly brought

A. J. Evans

S. E. Buckley

back to do their penance in the horrible circumstances of solitary confinement.

There was, of course, a considerable pool of escape experience at Ingolstadt and prisoners came to regard themselves as an 'Escaping Club', with one firm rule: they would all help each other plan and effect break-outs. Evans, on his own admission, was one of the less talented club members with, as he put it, 'no parlour tricks'. Nevertheless, he made attempts to escape, twice getting quite a distance from the Fort after sliding over the frozen moat. Both attempts failed, however, and so did the next scheme in which Evans was involved – tunnelling a way to freedom.

In fact, Evans never managed to escape from Ingolstadt. His chance came, ironically, when the Germans were moving Russian and English prisoners to new camps. In May 1917, Evans and Lieutenant Buckley, another prisoner, who had once tried to get out of Ingolstadt in a muck bin, were told they were to be sent to Zorndorf camp. This was an intolerable place, Buckley told Evans, and the two of them teamed up and began to plot an escape.

Ingolstadt is today a quiet, peaceful town north of Munich in West Germany

On the morning of 22nd May, 1917, Evans, Buckley and the other prisoners left the camp and were marched the 11 kilometres to Ingolstadt station. Evans and Buckley were nothing short of walking larders; they had quite a task to march normally with every pocket stuffed full of chocolate, biscuits, raw bacon, meat lozenges and tins of malted milk powder. In addition, Evans was carrying a large haversack full of food.

At Ingolstadt, the prisoners were settled in second class coaches with a sentry to guard each carriage. The train rattled the 110 kilometres to Nuremberg, where Evans and Buckley moved to the two corner seats near the window. It was dark, almost midnight, and the two escapers sat waiting tensely until the right moment arrived – when the train next slowed down.

At last, the train dropped speed as it passed through a pine forest. Evans and Buckley nodded to each other. Evans leaned across to the sentry and asked him, in German: 'Will you have some food? We are going to eat!' Before the sentry could answer, the other four prisoners in the carriage stood up and made a great business of obstructing each other as they pulled their haversacks from the racks above. For vital seconds, as planned, Evans and Buckley were obscured from the sentry. Swiftly, Evans slipped the strap of his haversack over his shoulder, pushed the carriage window down, slung a leg over and jumped. He landed by the side of the track in dark shadow. Buckley followed him about three seconds later. The two of them crouched down in a ditch as the train clanked off down the track, vanishing into the night. Silence: no shouts, no gunfire or other sounds of pursuit. The escape, this far, had succeeded.

The two men scrambled off down the side of the track and into the cool, damp quiet of the pine forest. They were, they reckoned, about 25 kilometres north of Nuremberg and 300 kilometres from their destination, the Swiss frontier. They had supplies, they had a compass and they had a map. They even had a stock of pepper with which to cover their tracks: sprinkled on the ground, the pepper would confuse any dogs their pursuers might use to sniff them out. They felt confident, all

the more so when they discovered they were enjoying that indispensible commodity, escapers' luck.

Evans and Buckley saw no-one for three days as they moved through the forests of Bavaria by night, crossing streams and skirting round towns and villages. Then, at about 9.00pm on the evening of 25th May, they made the mistake of being impatient to set off instead of waiting another half an hour for dusk. They were filling their water bottles from a stream by the side of the road when a man and a boy rode by on bicycles. Something made the cyclists stop and come over to them.

The man scrutinised the two Englishmen in the fading light. 'Auslander? Sie sind Aus-lander?' he asked warily.

Buckley gripped his thick walking stick and looked the German in the eye. 'No, we are *not* foreigners,' he replied loudly, in German. 'We are north Germans on a walking tour and have lost our way.'

'Nein, sie sind Auslander,' the man insisted.

The only thing to do was to show temper and impatience, an illogical but effective way to convince people they were wrong. Buckley did just that, shouting some very uncomplimentary things about the man's shocking Bavarian dialect. Then he stalked off, with Evans looking equally furious by his side.

Once they were out of sight, Evans and Buckley ran deep into the forest; behind them they could hear signs that they were being followed by men and dogs and they were constantly afraid that their pursuers would catch up with them. They sprinkled pepper

The two Englishmen jumping from the train into the dense forests of Bavaria

behind them as they ran and it was nearly midnight before they were satisfied that they were safe. After that, leaving their daytime hiding place too early was a mistake they did not repeat.

Lying low for 17 or 18 boiling hot, exhausting hours by day, they became more than ever cover-of-darkness creatures. Wherever they could, they followed railways or main roads, but the detours they had to make to avoid villages often took them deep into forests or out across barley fields. More than once, they found they were lost or had been tramping round in circles. Nevertheless, when they regained their bearings, the map and compass told them that they were steadily moving southwards.

The long, hard journey to freedom was, however, taking its toll. Night after night of tramping along stony railway lines, rough paths and dew-soaked fields had left their feet sore and bruised. Both men ached with weariness and when rainfall was sparse, they

gasped with thirst. Suffering such hardships, it was not surprising that by the time they had been on the run for a fortnight, Evans and Buckley looked thoroughly tattered. It was

Escape route taken by Evans and Buckley

astounding as well as fortuitous that the German with the scythe was stupid enough not to realise they were runaways when he challenged them on the evening of 5th June. At that perilous juncture, Evans and Buckley were only about 15 kilometres from the Swiss frontier: across more thick woods, more water meadows and a valley blanketed in thick mist.

Three days later, they lay on the edge of the wood, watching the sunset and waiting impatiently for nightfall. In front of them was a river and beyond that, 450 metres away, lay Switzerland. At last, by 10·15 pm it was dark; the moon would not rise for just under two hours. Evans and Buckley set out from the wood, crossed a railway and a road, and reached the water meadow beyond. They dropped to the ground and began to crawl on all fours through the long thick grass, which seemed to them to swish thunderously in the still darkness.

Suddenly, in the first faint glimmer of moonlight, Buckley spotted a sentry 15 metres away, walking along the footpath close to the stream. The two escapers froze, expecting at any moment to hear the dread shout of 'Alt!' and the sound of sentries thrashing their way through the meadow towards them. But the sentry passed by noticing nothing.

Quickly, Evans and Buckley splashed across the stream and up the bank the other side and, with a vigour they did not know they still possessed, pelted headlong for the frontier. One hundred metres, fifty, twenty, ten – and Evans was able to flash a quick look at a large notice board on a post; it marked the border five metres away. Then, as their feet crunched on the pebble-strewn path, the distance shrank to two metres, and a few seconds later they stepped over the border into Switzerland.

It was 12·30 pm on the morning of 9th June, 1917. After eighteen vagabond days, they were free.

Barzheim in Switzerland, a little village of no particular importance just over the border from Germany, but the first safe resting place for Evans and Buckley for many long days and nights

CHAPTER 12

The Priest who Helped Thousands Escape

To their amazement and rage, the Nazis saw their victim walk straight past without even glancing at the priest.

During 1943 and 1944, the one thing that most infuriated the Gestapo rulers of Rome was the sight of the tall, black-robed Irish priest standing night after night, waiting on the topmost step of the Vatican Basilica. The Gestapo troops could only look on from across the long piazza that lay between them, fingers itching at their triggers, longing to shoot him down. They watched as furtive figures scurried towards the Basilica and climbed the 22 steps to where the priest stood: a short, whispered exchange of information would take place and then, still in full view of the watching Gestapo, the figure would make off towards some hideout with that tense, loping gait common to all fugitives in fear of their lives.

The fugitive might be a British, French, Russian or other Allied prisoner of war escaped from captivity, a runaway Jew, an anti-Nazi Italian, a Yugoslav or Greek partisan – anyone, in fact, who was trying to elude capture, imprisonment and possible torture and death at Gestapo hands.

More than any of these numerous enemies of the Nazi Third Reich, the man the Gestapo most wanted to get their hands on was that priest – Monsignor Hugh Joseph O'Flaherty, officially, Notary in the Holy Office of the Vatican, unofficially, the most active and most successful single saviour of fugitives in the whole of Nazi-occupied Europe. On any one night, O'Flaherty had around 200 refugees hidden away in apartment blocks, villas, churches and other secret venues throughout Rome. On any one day, O'Flaherty and his fellow priests could be visiting runaways in

The beautiful colonnade in St. Peter's Square designed by Bernini in 1656

two dozen or more different places; the priest had the aid of countless Roman housewives, shopkeepers and apartment block porters.

The whole of Rome, it must have seemed to the furious Gestapo, was actively engaged in helping O'Flaherty or in preserving him from their clutches. It became close to a compulsion for the Gestapo to find some means of capturing the man. The main bar to their doing so lay in the fact that O'Flaherty operated from behind the dotted white line that separated the city of Rome from neutral papal territory in the Vatican. The Basilica, where he waited for escapers to seek his help, the Holy Office where he worked and the German College where he lived were all on this neutral and therefore untouchable ground.

One way to snatch O'Flaherty was for the Gestapo to arrest him on one of his frequent outings from the Vatican. On one occasion, Gestapo troops surrounded the building in Rome's *Via delle Corso* where O'Flaherty was visiting Prince Fillipo Doria Pamphili, one of several wealthy Romans who supplied him with money for his rescue work. The Prince

spotted the telltale uniforms of Gestapo men in the courtyard below, and O'Flaherty went hurtling down the stairs just as several of them began hammering on the Prince's front door. The priest rushed into the cellar where coal was being tipped down from the street above; he stripped off his cassock and crammed it into a coal sack together with his hat, rubbed dirt onto his face and hair and all over his shirt and chest, then climbed out of the coal-hole, a blackened, grimy figure. O'Flaherty threw the sack containing his clothes onto his back and walked straight past the Nazi guards in the street. He slipped round the other side of the coal truck, which hid him

A narrow escape for Father O'Flaherty as, disguised as a coalman, he walks past the Gestapo

114

from sight as he pelted across the road and round the nearest corner. The Gestapo apparently never worked out how the priest had managed to elude them.

Other equally unsuccessful moves were made to catch O'Flaherty by attempting to get people to betray him. Many times, the Gestapo tried to bribe members of O'Flaherty's household into helping them, but none would ever co-operate. Then, at last, the Gestapo seemed to be on the brink of success: they caught an old peasant and subjected him to such hideous tortures that simply to end his torment, the poor old man agreed to help lure O'Flaherty off Vatican territory.

The old man was sent off across the Basilica piazza to meet the priest and lead him into the grasp of a waiting Nazi squad. To their amazement and rage, the Nazis saw their victim walk straight past without even glancing at O'Flaherty. The peasant knew perfectly

well that the penalty for such brazen defaulting would be death and fortunately for him, O'Flaherty guessed what was going on. The peasant became one more fugitive for the priest to conceal.

O'Flaherty had never meant to set up his complex secret network which permeated Rome and involved the British Minister to the Vatican, Sir Francis Godolphin D'Arcy Osborne, several top level cardinals and at times, even Pope Pius XII himself. He had started out with the simple idea that as a Christian, his duty was to divide what comfort and aid he could to the victims of war.

Fascist Italy entered World War II on the side of Nazi Germany on 10th June, 1940 and by the following April, there were thousands of prisoners of war in Italian camps. O'Flaherty became one of two nuncios (messengers) appointed by Pope Pius to visit these men, provide warm clothing against the fierce Italian winter, hurry up delivery of Red Cross parcels and arrange for messages to be sent back home to let families and friends know that, although captive, the prisoners were still alive.

However, in the summer of 1943, large numbers of prisoners began escaping and arrived in Rome to claim the ecclesiastical sanctuary of the Vatican. The Vatican authorities had to be strictly neutral, and orders were given to the Swiss Guards who controlled the border of the Holy enclave that all fugitives were to be turned away. The Swiss soon learned to look the other way when necessary, and before long, the Vatican began to fill with a large assortment of absconders. The German College, for instance, was concealing refugee Jews, Italian aristocrats and Austrian professors as well as the escaped prisoners of war. Then, a fundamental change in Italy's position in the war converted this steady stream of fugitives into a flood. On 3rd September, 1943, Allied forces invaded Italy from the south. The Italian Government surrendered and a few days later declared war on their erstwhile Nazi ally. On 14th September, Nazi forces occupied Rome and set up a military government under the stern rule of the Gestapo.

Elsewhere in Italy, Italian camp guards

allowed thousands of prisoners to escape. Together with more prisoners hiding with the partisans in the hills of northern Italy, these men began to converge on Rome and the Vatican. Many were also converging on Monsignor O'Flaherty, whose kindness and energetic ways they had already seen when he was nuncio to their prison camps.

At first, O'Flaherty was able to send arrivals to his many personal friends in Rome, but he soon realised that only a proper escape organisation could deal with this problem, which was increasing in size daily as more and more runaways arrived at the Vatican's door.

As well as priests, padrones, messengers and lookouts, O'Flaherty was able to enlist the help of an escaped major in the Royal Artillery, Sam Derry. Derry dealt with everyday matters concerning the hideouts in Rome and, when necessary, it was his task to discipline the restless men forced to lie low in these hideouts for weeks on end. Sir D'Arcy Osborne 'lent' O'Flaherty his butler, the ingenious and enterprising John May, who was a master at manipulating black market supplies. It was May who managed to obtain forged documents, including passes enabling members of the organisation to be out on the streets after curfew and he who found a contact in the printing room of the Gestapo headquarters, which enabled O'Flaherty to receive a regular supply of copies of orders of the day giving details of planned raids on suspected hideouts.

There was, however, no means of obtaining warning of spontaneous, unrecorded Gestapo raids except, with luck, through messengers or porters who might raise the alarm mere minutes before the raiders arrived. It was these barely heralded strikes which posed the greatest peril for the padrones who were, in any case, in more constant danger than anyone else who helped O'Flaherty. If it became known they were harbouring escaped prisoners, they would be summarily executed; the unnerving experience of a Maltese widow, Mrs Henrietta Chevalier, showed how close that fate could be.

On the day in 1943 when the Gestapo suddenly burst in through Mrs Chevalier's front door, the five British soldiers she was

sheltering had no time to get out of the apartment. The Gestapo were already in the front hall when the soldiers were climbing over the balcony at the back; they hung from the railings while the apartment was searched and fortunately, although there were German soldiers down below, none looked up and saw them. Had they been spotted, then the five would, through no fault of their own, have broken the cardinal rule of those sheltered by the escape organisation: never to do anything that would let suspicion fall on the padrones who risked so much to give them refuge.

This was relatively easy to avoid when fugitives were 'confined to barracks', but it was less easy when they went for walks, to cafes or to the Rome Opera House in order to ease the boredom of their claustrophobic existence. Prisoners went out, of course, with

British fugitive 'Peter' desperately knocking down two Facists in an effort to avoid recapture

the necessary identification papers and in civilian clothes, but the danger of discovery went with them as well. Such a situation nearly caused disaster for one British officer, 'Peter' and for two padrones, Renzo and Adrienne Lucidi.

Peter took a girlfriend to a restaurant in Rome one evening just before Christmas 1943. As they left the restaurant and walked towards the tram stop, two members of the feared Gestapo slowly approached. Peter shoved the girl into a doorway and had walked a few yards past the Fascists when suddenly, they shouted out 'Documenti!' He showed them his papers, but the Fascists were not satisfied and produced their guns. Suddenly, Peter lunged at one Fascist and knocked the gun from his hand, pushed another one over and fled. Shots followed him as he hurtled round the nearest corner; he snaked his way through alleyways, doubled back and then back again until he thought he had shaken off his pursuers.

At that juncture, he was close to the apartment building in which Renzo and Adrienne Lucidi lived and without thinking, he dashed inside. By a wondrous stroke of luck, Adrienne Lucidi happened to be in the hallway as Peter pelted past. She realised at once what had happened, pushed Peter ahead of her into the lift and pressed the top floor button, sending the lift up just as the Fascists stormed into the hall. The porter, in suitably excited tones, told them their prey had just run out through the back entrance of the building. While they ran off on what they thought was a hot trail, Adrienne and Peter reached the top floor and got onto the roof, where Peter hid in a half-empty sand bin. Despite the porter's presence of mind and the success of his ruse, the Lucidi apartment was afterwards crossed off the list of hideouts. The mere fact that Peter had been seen running into their building was sufficient to make it too dangerous to use any more.

In any case, after Christmas 1943, the whole of Rome became more dangerous than ever. The perennially elusive O'Flaherty, the knowledge that British prisoners of war were defiantly walking the streets, the presence of communists, the proximity of Allied forces fighting their way towards Rome up the long 'leg' of Italy – all these factors served to increase the brutality and zeal of Gestapo efforts to clear the city of their enemies.

The Nazis embarked on a blitz of sudden raids in the first months of 1944 and arrested, among others, several of O'Flaherty's helpers, over 70 escaped prisoners and more than a dozen Italian padrones. Many of them were taken to the dreaded Regina Coeli prison, a place of terror where information was squeezed out of inmates by barbarous torture. Towards the end of March, five helpers in the escape organisation died in a Nazi reprisal for a communist ambush in which 32 German soldiers had been killed; they were among 320 hostages taken from Rome's prisons and massacred at the Ardeatine caves outside the city. The communists, undeterred, went on waging war against the Gestapo with bombs, gun fire and ambushes, making the streets perilous for O'Flaherty's priests as they went on their rounds visiting the hideouts.

118

Monsignor Hugh O'Flaherty, the 'Scarlet Pimpernel' of the Vatican, who like the famous fictitious hero of the French Revolution helped thousands escape from prison and death

Crowds celebrating in St. Peter's Square

It also made the Nazis extra alert and disaster seemed imminent for O'Flaherty when, in early May, a Dutch priest, Father Anselmo Musters, was arrested and taken for interrogation to Gestapo headquarters. For three weeks, Musters was beaten and threatened by the Gestapo and he was then thrown into a dark, dank, isolated cell for another fortnight. At the very beginning, the Gestapo had shown Musters a diagram which revealed that they knew almost everything there was to know about O'Flaherty's network: even a morsel of additional information could have shattered the whole system. In order to salvage as much as possible, Major Derry arranged to clear all the hiding places on Musters' round. He need not have bothered. Musters told the Gestapo nothing and after five weeks, they gave up.

Musters was put on a train bound for a concentration camp in Germany where, as he well knew, the only prospect was death. With nothing to lose, he waited for an opportunity to escape. His chance came when the train stopped for a few hours outside Florence and his handcuffs were removed for him to eat his meal. Musters wriggled through the window of his carriage and ran off down the

track. Later, he returned to Rome, where he arrived ragged and exhausted, to find that the British, Americans and French had already entered the city and freed it on 4th June, 1944.

In the previous few days of that month, Allied forces had fought their way nearer and nearer to Rome, and the Germans still there had pulled out, fleeing northward by the truck-load. Early on the morning of 4th June, a Sunday, the peal of bells from Rome's 400 churches triumphantly proclaimed the news that Allied troops were in the city. Thousands of Romans swarmed into St Peter's Square cheering, crying, dancing and hugging each other in a ferment of joy and relief. While all Rome celebrated its liberation and nearly 4,000 fugitives poured from their hideouts to join in, the man to whom they owed their lives was alone. Monsignor O'Flaherty was in a small chapel, on his knees, praying.

CHAPTER 13

Operation Shetland Bus

The fishing boat had rounded a bend in a narrow channel, making for the pick-up point, when she was confronted at point-blank range with German guns.

There is especial valour in escaping from danger, then risking new-found safety to return to the aid of those who have been left behind. During World War II, many fishermen and merchant seamen from Norway did just this; they escaped across the North Sea to Britain after the Nazi invasion in April 1940 and then volunteered to go back on missions for the rescue and supply route known as Operation Shetland Bus.

The missions had many purposes, all of them vital to the Norwegians' hopes of surviving the depredations of their Nazi conquerors. The Norwegian underground movement needed weapons, ammunition, explosives, radio operators and sabotage experts to help them wage effective secret war against the Nazis. The fishing vessels of Operation Shetland Bus supplied all of these, sailing from the Shetland Isles across the North Sea with equipment and personnel hidden away in their fish holds or concealed under piles of fishing nets and other tackle. Operation Shetland Bus was also involved in rescue missions, dispatching boats to pick up refugees and other fugitives from lonely creeks on the fjord-fringed coast.

Needless to say, operating the Shetland Bus was exceedingly dangerous and the chances of detection and disaster were very high. All

Aksel sailing out of the harbour at Lunna Voe on the first 'bus' voyage

the same, in the summer of 1941, when news of the venture first spread around the Norwegian community in London, the British organisers, Major L. H. Mitchell and Lieutenant-Commander David Howarth were besieged by dozens of seamen clamouring to join.

The Norwegians' eagerness was understandable. London was a tedious place for tough, fearless men more attuned to the challenging freedom of seafaring life than to sitting out the war in some safer, softer niche. The Shetland Isles, at the extreme north-east corner of Britain, was in any case a place where Norwegians would feel more at home than they did among the sophistications of a capital city. The islanders, like themselves, were descendants of Norse Vikings. The bleak, craggy islands with their shores indented with creeks, the mists, the ice-blue skies and the clear bright sunlight of near-Arctic latitudes —

all this mirrored closely the west coast of Norway some 130 kilometres and 24 hours' journey away. This Norwegian coastline was to be the objective, and sometimes the battleground, of Operation Shetland Bus.

The 'busmen' who made the first foray there were the crew of the 20-metre twin-masted fishing vessel *Aksel*, skippered by August Naeroy with Mindur Berge as engineer. On 30th August, 1941, *Aksel* sailed out of harbour at Lunna Voe in the east Shetlands and crossed the North Sea to Bergen. On board was an agent carrying important information for a group of local underground fighters. The agent was landed without incident and the boat aroused such scant attention that Naeroy, Burge and the rest of the crew were able to go to a local dance. *Aksel* returned to Lunna Voe on 5th September.

Further trips in the first half of September, none of which attracted Nazi attention or met with trouble, landed the first supplies of weapons, ammunition and bombs for the secret army of Norwegian resistance fighters, brought ten refugees to safety at Lerwick and even provided a wife for one of the skippers, Ingvald Johansen: she accompanied him on his return journey and married him in Aberdeen soon after their arrival.

All the same, no-one at Lunna Voe was rash enough to be lulled by the ease of the first few voyages, which had taken place on the edge of autumn when the notoriously treacherous North Sea was still in fairly reasonable mood. This luxury was not going to last.

Operation Shetland Bus was essentially a wintertime effort, for then, greatest use could be made of the long, impenetrably black northern nights. At the same time, utmost skill would be required to navigate the dangerous, winter sea, where sudden violent gales could whip up the water into mountainous waves and smash the wooden decks of fishing boats to splintered fragments.

Sooner or later, too, the Germans in Norway would realise that something was going on and that the common sight of fishing boats spreading their nets offshore might not be as innocent as it seemed. Once German suspicions were aroused, and once they acted upon them, a boat could be bombed out of the water by an aircraft in only two or three low-flying runs, torpedoed by a U-boat or sunk by one of the artillery batteries lining the Norwegian coast. Or, most insidious of all, a Norwegian collaborator – a quisling, as such traitors were called – could alert the Germans' attention.

Towards the end of September, 1941, Operation Shetland Bus experienced its first problems when two fishing boats, *Aksel* and *Vita*, became seriously overdue. *Vita* had left Lunna Voe on 22nd September to pick up a party of refugees near Trondheim. She was due back on 28th September, but two days later, there was no sign of her. Meanwhile, *Aksel* had set off to retrieve a second group of Trondheim refugees, this time from Traena Island which lay inside the Arctic Circle.

Aksel had been gone three or four days when Major Mitchell received chilling news, in a coded telegram from London. Information had filtered through from Norway that a ship, numbered SS-18-F, had been seized by the Germans. It was the *Vita*: that had been the fake number specially painted on her hull. Forewarned of the escape bid, the Germans had had a warship waiting for *Vita* when she arrived; the fishing boat had rounded a bend in a narrow channel, making for the pick-up point, when she was confronted at point-blank range with German guns. Against their murderous firepower, *Vita* had no chance. In seconds, she was wrecked and though Ingvald Johansen and his three-man crew survived, they were captured and spent the rest of the war in a German prison camp.

The refugees whose escape had been foiled managed to get away. However, German knowledge of their attempt put the other Shetland boat, *Aksel*, in grave danger. *Aksel*'s party of refugees came from the same organisation in Trondheim. Did the Germans also know about *them*?

When the *Vita* was destroyed, *Aksel* was still en route to Norway, and Major Mitchell made desperate efforts to warn skipper August Naeroy and his crew that they might be sailing into an ambush. At that time, the fishing boats had not yet been fitted with two-way radio and the only hope of making contact was to send out an aircraft.

On the afternoon of 30th September, a Royal Air Force Sunderland flying boat took off from the Shetlands to search the area where *Aksel* should have been, about 960 kilometres from Traena Island. Mitchell was appalled when the Sunderland returned in the evening to report nothing but empty sea. Next day, a Catalina flying boat made another search, but it, too, found no trace of *Aksel*.

There was nothing to do now but watch, wait, hope and pray. Mitchell and Lieutenant-Commander Howarth were so profoundly anxious that they spent day after day standing on the cliffs above Lunna Voe with the icy winds of the northern autumn whipping around them, keeping watch for *Aksel*. Night after night, the two of them remained half-awake, listening for the familiar 'tonking' throb of *Aksel*'s 100hp engine. As the days passed and the vigil continued, hope began to fade and crews setting out on further trips to Norway did so in tense and depressed mood.

Then, at last, on the night of 10th October, a faint throbbing sound was heard far out to sea. All over Lunna Voe, men strained their ears as the sound grew louder. Mitchell, Howarth and a crowd of Norwegians pelted down to the quay and peered into the darkness where, suddenly, looming out of the murk, they saw the prow of *Aksel*. August Naeroy and the rest of *Aksel*'s crew were almost too exhausted and disgruntled to respond to the cheering and back-slapping that greeted them as they came ashore.

It was understandable, for they had a dismal

story to tell. Bad luck had dogged their mission from the first. Storm, fog and a faulty compass had delayed them, and when they did arrive at Traena, their cargo of refugees was nowhere to be seen. Apparently, they had been scared away by the Gestapo, who had scoured the island the week before. Furious at their wasted journey, *Aksel*'s crew decided to return to the Shetlands. They were two days out to sea when they sighted the periscope of a U-boat close by. For three hours, until darkness and thick fog descended, the U-boat tracked the fishing boat. When dawn came, the periscope had fortunately disappeared, but shortly afterwards, the main bearing of *Aksel*'s engine failed. It took two days' gruelling work in stormy seas to repair it.

Similar tales of danger and difficulty were told time and again over the next four winters as a succession of boats battled to and from Norway, braving storms and high seas, and slipping under the noses of German coastal patrols to snatch refugees from the hostile shore or deliver dangerous cargoes of munitions on remote and lonely beaches.

Typical of the dangers endured by ships and volunteers, and some refugees, was the series of events that brought the *Siglaos* limping back to Lerwick riddled with bullet holes, her sails reduced to rags, the mizzen-mast almost sliced through and with one of her crew dead.

Siglaos, skippered by a merchant seaman called Gundersen, landed an agent near the village of Oklandsvaag towards the end of October, 1941. While the boat was in harbour, a local doctor begged Gundersen to take away a party of seven refugees who were in grave danger of arrest. Gundersen agreed, stowed the refugees in the ship's cabin and set sail just before midnight on 27th October. A savage north-west gale was blowing and it so impeded *Siglaos*' progress that when dawn broke, the boat was no more than 80 kilometres from the Norwegian coast.

Forewarned of Vita's journey the Germans lie in wait and destroy her

The first thing crew and passengers saw in the grey early morning light was the very last thing they wanted: a twin-engined German aircraft was approaching from the south. *Siglaos'* deck was still bucking in wild seas; there was neither time nor opportunity to get to the antitank rifles and other guns, which had been lashed down for security below decks, before the aircraft zoomed over at mast height and slaked the length of the boat with cannon fire. Skipper Gundersen and Bard Grotle, the engineer, wasted no more time; they rushed to the cabin to get the guns, but before they could do so, the aircraft swooped over again, spitting more fire from its nose and tail. On the aircraft's third run, Grotle met it with a blazing Tommy-gun; he emptied a whole magazine in the aircraft's direction before it circled round and made off eastwards.

All the time this had been going on, a young crewman, Nils Nesse, had remained on deck trying to control the wheel. Afterwards, he was found slumped unconscious with bullets in his head and leg. One of the refugees, a nurse, looked after him as best she could, but Nesse died an hour later. *Siglaos* struggled back into Lerwick some two days afterwards.

Crews and refugees of many other boats did not survive to tell of the disasters that overtook them. One such boat, the 17-metre *Blia*, disappeared on her way back to the Shetlands in a wild storm in November 1941. Crammed on board were about 40 refugees, most of them escaping from the Gestapo. They all perished, as did *Blia's* crew, but no-one ever knew for certain what had happened. There were only the dismal possibilities: the boat might have broken up in the heaving seas or was, perhaps, flooded by a giant wave and capsized.

In 1942, the year in which the Nazis captured a Shetland bus crew in uniform and shot them all without trial, Per Blystad and Mindur Berge set off in an eight-metre open boat, the *Sjo*, to reconnoitre the Norwegian coastal defences. They never returned. Quite probably, both of them were captured and executed.

At the end of the same year, the *Aksel* went down in yet another savage storm and her entire crew, Bard Grotle among them, was

a bomb. Shortly afterwards, a Hardanger cutter, the *Feie*, sailed for Bergen in unseasonally calm weather and vanished. No wreckage. No message for help. And, even later, no news of what had occurred.

The loss of these ships and crews within weeks of each other reduced the manpower of Operation Shetland Bus from 60 to only 36. But there were always more Norwegians to be found in wartime Britain willing to volunteer as replacements. Between September 1941 and the end of the war in May, 1945, the Shetland fishing boats, none of them more

Siglaos bucking in the wild seas, trying to avoid the attacks of the German aircraft

than about 20 metres long, made journeys totalling 145,000 kilometres, rescued 350 refugees, established sixty radio transmitters in Norway, landed dozens of agents, and armed and equipped thousands of Norwegian partisans and saboteurs.

lost. Three weeks later, in January 1943, the *Sandoy* disappeared; she had a cargo of high explosives on board and rumour subsequently had it that a German aircraft attacked the boat and ignited her cargo with

This work, performed by men who, had they wished, could have remained safe and free in Britain, gave rise to a new phrase in Norway's wartime vocabulary: 'Taking the Shetland Bus' was widely used there as a synonym for last minute rescue and escape from overwhelming danger, and also for succour in the fight against Nazi tyranny.

CHAPTER 14

Napoleon's Last Victory

*It was the best
'cover' for escape that Napoleon
could have wished for: the idiot image he
had cunningly publicised had lulled
Europe into euphoria.*

In 1814, when the British frigate *Undaunted* landed Napoleon Bonaparte into exile at Portoferraio, Elba, the crew sent him a farewell message. It was friendly, but spiced with a certain impudence:

'Long life and prosperity on the island of Elba. Better luck next time!'

Napoleon, by all accounts, received it with a wry, bitter smile. Not so long before, the men who sent that greeting were chilled by the very name of Napoleon Bonaparte, Emperor of the French. Not so long before, Napoleon had seemed poised to conquer their islands and make them part of his great empire, which stretched down into Italy and eastwards across Europe into Poland. Napoleon was Europe's greatest conqueror since the Romans.

Not any more. With his defeat at the battle of Leipzig in October, 1813, Napoleon's seventeen-year run of brilliant military success had come to an end and his victorious enemies packed him off to Elba, a tiny island backwater in the Mediterranean.

Ostensibly, Napoleon was still an Emperor – he had abdicated as Emperor of the French, but was allowed to keep the title – but his 'empire' was now the 222 square kilometres of Elba. His new 'subjects' – he was once the autocrat of millions – were the 12,000 people who inhabited the island. Napoleon's 'army' now consisted of a few hundred men, a remnant compared to the thousands he had once commanded on no less than 60 battle-fields. His 'navy' was one solitary brig, *Inconstant*, and a few small feluccas (oared coasting vessels).

When a man of such stature had fallen as far from the peak of power and glory as Napoleon had by 1814, it was no wonder that a group of humble British seamen felt sufficiently safe to bid him a cheery but impertinent farewell.

The crew of H.M.S. *Undaunted* could hardly fail to realise what all Europe knew, namely that Napoleon's new domain was little more than a shabby front barely obscuring the shame of his downfall. His circumstances were, in reality, humiliating. Elba was thick with spies planted to watch and report on his every move. A British commissioner, Sir Neil Campbell, was in residence to keep a wary eye on all that went on and Napoleon's correspondence was scrutinised by the French 'Cabinet Noir', the censorship service.

The reasons for such extreme precautions were fear, suspicion and the knowledge that in making him 'Emperor of Elba', Napoleon's enemies had cut him down to far less than his real size. It was ludicrous to suppose that this remarkable figure of the French Revolution had leapt from obscurity as the son of a Corsican lawyer to create and dominate a vast empire, only to settle for an undemanding life as ruler of a small island. Napoleon was one of those rarities in history: a charismatic leader of genius, and the ardour and awe he could create were very evident on the afternoon of 4th May, 1814, when he went ashore at Portoferraio.

As the barge carrying Napoleon made its way to the jetty, small craft rowed out, loaded with people throwing flowers into the water. Guns fired salutes for minutes on end. Musicians played. Choirs sang. Elbans cheered and waved handkerchiefs from the quayside, from every window and balcony and from the battlements of forts overlooking the harbour. The Mayor of Portoferraio was there to present Napoleon with the keys of the town on a silver plate, and as he proceeded from the jetty into the town, four men held over Napoleon's head a canopy of gilt and wood specially constructed for the occasion.

Napoleon's arrival on Elba. The chief dignitaries of the island turned out to welcome the emperor, who, in spite of his captivity, was still regarded by everyone as a person of international importance

The people of Elba were clearly overawed by Napoleon and were all set to treat him with the utmost deference. At first, or so the spies on Elba presumed, Napoleon responded with a fatherly concern for the Elbans' welfare and showed encouraging signs of settling down. He found himself a house at Portoferraio, which he turned into a splendidly furnished, gilded and painted palace. He took a summer villa at San Martino and from time to time occupied other residences, which he fitted out in a suitably elegant style. He established a stable of horses and kept a number of carriages for travelling about the island. He gave dinner parties for local dignitaries and balls for prominent citizens.

It all seemed to indicate that Napoleon was, after all, prepared to live the leisured life of an affluent emigré. But defeat at Leipzig and exile on Elba had done nothing to quench his ambition or his energy. Elba was, in any case, far too close to Europe – only 11 kilometres from the coast of Italy and three days' sail from the South of France – for Napoleon to lose interest in what was going on across the water. He was, in fact, watching events very closely. He had his own spies and gleaned information from visiting Britons, Germans and other foreigners.

By the end of 1814, much of the news which was reaching Napoleon was extremely encouraging. The allies who had combined against him – Britain, Austria, Russia and Prussia – were quarrelling among themselves, and at the Congress of Vienna, where they met in September 1814, there were protracted boundary disputes, wrangles about resettling the former French imperial lands and numerous other international clashes. In France itself, the new Bourbon king, Louis XVIII, was making himself thoroughly unpopular. With incredible stupidity, Louis was trying to restore absolute royal rule, the same mode of government bloodily overthrown by the French Revolution of 1789. Napoleon heard with some pleasure that Louis's military guard

A romantic study of Napoleon as a young man, painted in 1796 by the French historical painter Baron Antoine Gros. The portrait now hangs in the Louvre in Paris

did their duties in sullen, resentful fashion, and civilians were becoming restive.

Less comforting, however, were the rumours coming from Vienna of plans to deport Napoleon to the West Indies, to the Azores, 1,100 kilometres out in the Atlantic, or to an even more remote place, the coaling station of St Helena. There were other problems, too. Napoleon had good reason to fear attempts to kill him on Elba, and early in 1815, a visiting delegation of Germans apparently urged him 'to take the fullest precautions, as three hired assassins had been sent to Portoferriao'. What was more, Napoleon's expenses on Elba were so great that the personal fund of four million francs he brought with him was soon running out: the new French government had promised him a subsidy of two million francs, but it had not arrived. If Napoleon's finances shrank so much that he had to reduce his already tiny army, it would be impossible for him to resist should attempts be made to remove him.

All these dangers and difficulties combined with news of disunity in Europe and discontent in France to convince Napoleon that he must escape from Elba. France, it seemed clear, badly needed him and he was sure Europe would once more bend to his will. A high degree of discretion and deception was going to be required, though. Napoleon had to escape and land in France with large numbers of men, not an easy proceeding to arrange in secret. And the ever-present bevy of spies teeming about him were watching more closely than ever for signs that he meant to abscond.

One of the most diligent snoopers on Elba was known variously as Alessandro Forli or the 'Olive Oil Merchant'. The commerce acted as his 'cover'. Forli reported regularly to the Chevalier Mariotti, the French consul in Leghorn, and with his carefully cultivated connections among Napoleon's close associates, he proved a reliable and valuable spy. In December 1814, Forli told Mariotti of two significant remarks that had come to his ears. Napoleon, Forli said, had commented: 'Would it be too soon to leave the island during the Carnival?' – the Mardi Gras due to take place in February – and 'I see it will be necessary to take the field again'. Mariotti received this news with great alarm and had warning sent to the French government in Paris: Napoleon was thinking of escape!

Then, to confuse everyone, Forli's reports gave information that appeared to contradict this conclusion. Napoleon was very friendly with the British commissioner, Sir Neil Campbell, and so charmed him that Campbell became

The elaborate and colourful Mardi Gras carnival on Elba is still held every year

convinced the Emperor had no thought of leaving Elba. Campbell was so sure of it that he applied to be relieved of his post on the island. He was persuaded to change his mind when to the astonishment of all, Napoleon specifically asked him to stay. The Emperor, everyone now concluded, was *not* thinking of escape. This idea appeared to be confirmed when, at the start of 1815, Napoleon concerned himself with opening a new theatre on Elba and masterminding the February Mardi Gras. These were activities of such extraordinary frivolity that Napoleon's enemies began to wonder if he had lost his wits.

At the Mardi Gras carnival on 15th February, the spies on Elba reported to their astounded masters that Napoleon dressed up soldiers as pierrots. He had his commander of the Guard swathe himself in a shawl and pretend to be a Turkish pasha. The pasha's 'harem' consisted of guardsmen in veils, travelling in procession in cardboard floats, throwing flowers at the crowds and trying to laugh in suitably coquettish voices.

After this, a red-faced Mariotti was told he was crazy to talk of an escape from Elba. Napoleon the Conqueror had clearly become Napoleon the Clown. Cartoons and caricatures began to spread this idea round the Continent, showing the Emperor as a fat, senile dodderer. It was the best 'cover' for escape that Napoleon could have wished for: the idiot image he had cunningly publicised had lulled Europe into euphoria.

King Louis XVIII's ministers, the French police and the postal censors were all so convinced that Napoleon was now a decrepit half-wit that they discounted the significance of letters that began to come out of Elba on 6th February. In an unsigned letter, which the censors intercepted, information was requested about Colonel de la Bedoyère, an ardent supporter of Napoleon: had he yet taken up his post commanding regiments at Chambery, near Grenoble? The French Minister of Police dismissed it as inconsequential, filed it and forgot it. Another letter, dated 23rd February, and also read by the censors, made vague references to an imminent sally from Elba and the chance of finding aid in Grenoble. Incredibly, this, too, was ignored, but by the time the censors read it, it was already too late to stop Napoleon's escape. For on 23rd February, Napoleon sealed off the island. No ships were allowed in or out, not even fishing vessels. Troops were confined to barracks. The Elba police were forbidden to issue any passports.

Napoleon had seized the chance given him by the fortuitous absence of Sir Neil Campbell. Campbell, the only Allied official on Elba, had sailed to Leghorn on 16th February in *Partridge*, the only Allied patrol ship still on the Elba station. *Partridge* was not even out of sight before Napoleon ordered the brig *Inconstant* to be refitted, armed with 26 guns and made ready to go to sea within nine days. On 20th February, while work on *Inconstant* was proceeding, two cargo vessels, the *Mouche* and the *Abeille*, berthed at Portoferraio. After their cargoes were unloaded, Napoleon commandeered them as troop transports. Another ship, *Saint Esprit*, which took shelter at Portoferraio after being caught in a storm, was also detained in harbour.

By Sunday morning, 26th February, all was ready. 500 grenadiers would all travel aboard *Inconstant* and the two cargo ships would hold 600 troops between them, together with the baggage and the ammunition Napoleon required. *Saint Esprit* was to carry three of Napoleon's carriages, his silverware and other valuables.

Napoleon's departure from Elba was as emotional as his arrival. His freedom, however, was to be short-lived and ended at Waterloo

Soon after breakfast, Napoleon appeared at the usual Sunday gathering of notables, the 'levee', and announced he was leaving. It took only a short while for the news to spread all over the island and to reach the ears of Alessandro Forli. Forli was frantic. With the island sealed off from the outside world, he had no way of warning Mariotti in Leghorn, or anyone else. In desperation, Forli bribed a boatman to take him off the island in his small sailing craft, but the boat was only a little way across the harbour before a sentry on *Inconstant* ordered it back to the quay at the point of his rifle. Forli was left to fume in total frustration.

At 5 o'clock that evening, Napoleon's troops began to march down to the quayside and embark on the ships. They were watched by a silent, sad-faced crowd. Napoleon arrived as it was getting dark, to find the Mayor too tearful to deliver his farewell greetings and the ramparts of the forts lined with lanterns held by the dozens of Elbans who had come from all over the island to witness his departure. Napoleon paused to scan the scene, then embraced the weeping Mayor and stepped into *Inconstant*'s longboat.

*Leader of the French once more, Napoleon is carried
shoulder high into the palace of the Tuileries*

Napoleon's fleet sailed from Portoferraio
on a favourable southerly wind and three
days later, on 1st March, 1815, he landed in
the South of France at Golfe Juan.

By then, Sir Neil Campbell had returned
from Leghorn to receive an appalling shock.
As he sailed into Portoferraio, he saw that
Inconstant was not there. Neither were
Napoleon's grenadiers: their guard posts had
been taken over by the Elban militia. Princess
Pauline Borghese, Napoleon's sister, was still
on the island and Campbell raged and cursed
and tried to threaten her into saying where
the Emperor had gone. She told him nothing.
Campbell was forced to return to his ship, set
sail with all speed and scour the Mediterranean
for his missing captive.

When the infuriated Campbell found Napoleon's ships, they were empty. Napoleon and his men had already disembarked and were on their triumphant way to Grenoble, Lyons and finally, having gathered 14,000 men on the way, to Paris. King Louis XVIII fled, convinced that another revolution had begun. Next day, 20th March, Napoleon was carried shoulder high into the royal palace of the Tuileries by wildly cheering Parisians.

Their joy was, however, short lived. So was their certainty that Napoleon would restore the heady days of French revolutionary grandeur. Napoleon's last fling at glory, the so-called Hundred Days, ended on 18th June, 1815, with his defeat by British and Prussian forces at the battle of Waterloo. Louis XVIII returned to the fury of the French. Napoleon, to their sorrow, was forced to abdicate a second time, and on 10th August, he set sail for permanent island exile in St Helena.

Only half the size of Elba, St Helena was even more of a backwater and very much more remote. It lay 2,000 kilometres west of the African coast out in the south Atlantic. From there, there could be no escape.

CHAPTER 15
Third Time Lucky

*Harrer knew that without
the rucksack his chances of survival
were virtually nil.*

As far as anyone could tell, the group of men looked just like an ordinary working party going about the everyday business of repairing the posts around the prison camp. Two of them were obviously British officers, complete with swagger canes. The other five were just as obviously Indians, with their dark skins, turbans and white robes. The British sergeant-major who rode by on a bicycle scarcely gave the working party a glance as they tramped across the dusty compound of the prison camp near Dehra Dun in northern India, heading for the main gate. The guards on duty at the gate gave the two officers a smart salute as they marched through. The officers nodded briskly in acknowledgement.

This, however, was the dangerous moment. If one of those guards noticed that the five Indians had Teutonic blue eyes or their dark Indian-looking make-up ran and stained their white clothes, then that would be the abrupt and instant end of their escape. But nothing happened. Neither of the guards noticed anything. They just stood there on that late

*The Germans coolly walking out of imprisonment
in India in April 1944*

April afternoon in 1944, unaware that the oldest trick in the annals of escape was being played upon them, and let the party of carefully disguised Germans and Austrians walk out of the camp unchallenged, down the path and out of sight round the corner and into the bushes.

It had all seemed incredibly easy, but at least one of the 'Indians', the Austrian skier and mountaineer Heinrich Harrer, knew how great were the risks and hardships of the next step in their escape. For Heinrich Harrer had tried to get away from Dehra Dun before, in May 1943, and had managed to remain free for eighteen days before he was caught. Now, a year later, as he hastily removed his white robes and dumped them in the bushes, he knew precisely what lay ahead of him.

The only escape route with a chance of success lay through the tangled forests, rushing rivers and tricky paths of the Himalayan foothills, where turning a corner could bring a man face to face with tigers, leopards or bears. Beyond the foothills lay the most demanding mountain country in the world, the ice-cold, merciless peaks of Tibet, with their savage winds, perilously narrow ledges and the great gaping chasms that waited to claim climbers at a stumble or the slip of a foot.

No wonder the Italian General Marchese, who had escaped with Harrer in 1943, had chosen not to try again. When the two of them were caught, at the nomad village of Nelang, 2,100 metres up in the mountains and about 160 kilometres from the Tibetan border,

Marchese had been so exhausted by extreme heat and gruelling effort that he had to be taken back to Dehra Dun on horseback. Even Harrer, who was fitter than Marchese and, at 31, about ten years younger, had arrived back at the camp in a distinctly weakened state, thin and gaunt from hunger and fatigue and the rigours both of them had had to endure.

Harrer's emaciated appearance was not, however, matched by a similarly weakened will. The desire to escape was still as strong as

137

it had been on 3rd September, 1939, when within minutes of World War II being declared, Harrer had found himself no longer a welcome foreign visitor to British India, but an enemy alien to be taken into custody. Escape and the means of escape had occupied his mind from that moment, and Harrer had, in fact, made a brief bid for freedom not long after his arrest.

It had happened while he and other enemy aliens were being transferred by lorry from one camp to another. As the lorry negotiated a corner, throwing up clouds of choking, all-concealing dust, Harrer and another man called Lobenhoffer jumped off and sprinted twenty metres down the road towards the surrounding jungle. Harrer tumbled into a ditch behind a bush, only to see, to his dismay, that the whole convoy had ground to a halt. Indian guards blew warning whistles and shot rifles into the air, and a group of them surrounded Lobenhoffer, presenting him with a ring of menacing bayonets. Lobenhoffer had been carrying the rucksack and without that, Harrer knew his chances of survival were virtually nil.

Nevertheless, Harrer determined that there would be other chances and even the failure of his escape with General Marchese in May 1943, did not deter him from trying again.

Harrer had, in fact, prepared the ground for a third escape bid even before he and Marchese had been taken back to Dehra Dun. While waiting at a farmhouse for an escort to accompany them, Harrer had entrusted his maps, compass and money to a friendly Indian guard, knowing how impossible it would be to smuggle them back into the camp. Harrer arranged with the Indian that one night the following May, in 1944, he would return and collect these indispensable aids to escape. The Indian solemnly promised to wait for Harrer and care for his belongings.

During the next year, Heinrich Harrer thought of little else but the day when he would return to the farmhouse. Both he and Marchese spent four weeks in solitary confinement as punishment for their escape, which gave Harrer plenty of leisure to ruminate about the experience and decide where he had gone wrong.

His first conclusion was that taking a companion – even such a game and gallant one as Marchese – had been a mistake. Next time, he would make his way towards Tibet alone. A second mistake had been to pass through Nelang when the village was already inhabited by the nomads who lived there only in the summer months. Next time, Harrer determined he would plan his escape so that he reached Nelang before the nomads arrived. That way, there would be fewer people about and fewer Indians patrolling the area on police and border duties.

painted dark brown, his head shaved and wound with a turban and his khaki dress covered with a long, loose white robe.

Once beyond the main gate and out of sight of the guards, the 'working party' wasted no time. Brief, low-voiced farewells were exchanged and the group then split up. After running for a few miles with one of the 'officers', Harrer struck out on his own, up into the hills that would lead him along the route he and Marchese had taken the previous year, through the valleys of the rivers Jumna and Aglar. As Harrer already knew, this was the best and safest way. It was very far from being the easiest.

Harrer and Lobenhoffer trapped in India at the declaration of war make a bid for freedom

April 29th, 1944, close to the start of the 'escape season', was a date that would afford Harrer good chances of achieving that important objective. That day, Harrer and several other would-be escapers met in a hut to be turned into 'British officers' and 'Indians'. Harrer, like the other 'Indians', had his skin

Harrer spent the first night of his escape threading his way along narrow, stone-strewn trails, squeezing past clefts between boulders and wading through the river as it meandered along the valley and across his route. He progressed slowly and laboriously in switchback fashion, alternately climbing steep slopes and then making his way down into ravines, then up again, with each summit affording a vista of yet another ravine and another slope

139

beyond. But gradually, Harrer was moving upwards into the Himalayas and when the morning of 30th April dawned, he was exhausted, scratched and bruised, but pleased: that morning, as he eased himself into a day-time resting place between two boulders in the river bed, Harrer reflected that in one night he had covered as much ground as had taken four days with Marchese the year before. The going had been so tough, though, that Harrer found he had worn right through the soles of his new tennis shoes.

Harrer was thankful to rest that day, despite a group of apes who spotted him and pelted him with lumps of mud. As soon as darkness came again, he set off once more and two nights later, approached his first great hurdle: Mount Nag Tibba, more than 3,000 metres high, with its upper regions smothered in thick, uninhabited and dangerous forest.

It was here, on one of the mountain ridges, just as dawn was lighting the sky, that Harrer came face to face with a leopard. The animal sat on a branch four metres above the ground, staring in a baleful but intense way, flicking its tail and limbering up, Harrer was certain, to spring down upon him. To run might be fatal, to show fear would definitely be so. Harrer walked on as nonchalantly as he could, his hand gripping his only weapon, a long knife sheathed in a stick, and his skin tingling with terror. But mercifully, the leopard just watched, his interest unaroused.

Two nights later, Harrer reached the River Ganges, the great holy river of India. Nearby was the town of Uttar Kashi, which was filled with temples for devout Hindus on pilgrimage to this sacred region. Harrer was just making his way through the narrow streets, past the open temple doors where eerily glowing oil lamps lit up rows of idols, when two men suddenly rushed out at him, shouting and waving their arms. Harrer fled, scrambling across the fields, through the scrub and flinging himself into hiding between two boulders. He lay there for several minutes, not knowing whether his pursuers had been chasing away an unwelcome stranger, or whether news of the escape from Dehra Dun had put them on the lookout for Harrer and his fellow prisoners.

At last, the shouting and the noise of the chase died down, and Harrer was able to creep away. The experience made him very wary, however. As he approached the farm-house where he fervently hoped the Indian guard he had befriended the year before would be waiting for him, as arranged, he moved with extreme caution. Betrayal was not im-possible. Nor was the fact that the prison camp authorities had anticipated Harrer's moves and were lying in wait for him.

Harrer hid himself in the pool of darkness offered by the surrounding bushes and scanned the farmhouse and the paths and trees around it. Standing there, serene in the moonlight, it certainly looked quiet enough. Harrer listened for several minutes to see if the crack of a twig, the creak of a branch being pushed aside, or the crunch of a furtive foot on the path might betray hidden human presence. But there was nothing. At last, Harrer was reasonably satisfied, but as a final precaution, he hid his rucksack under the bushes. If by any chance things went wrong at the farm-house and he had to make a run for it, he could at least retrieve that. He began to creep

Leopards, like other cats, will usually not attack humans if they are neither hungry nor threatened

140

from one dark shadow to the next until he reached the farmhouse stable. Once there, he slipped inside and eased the door shut. Lowering his voice, he hissed out the Indian's name. Silence. Harrer called again, risking a slightly louder tone.

The name had hardly left his lips this second time before there was a rush of running feet outside and the door crashed open. There in the doorway stood the Indian, crying and gesticulating with joy. Suddenly, he threw himself down on the ground and kissed Harrer's feet, babbling out rapid greetings. At this extraordinary welcome, any residual thoughts of betrayal or ambush vanished from Harrer's mind.

A few minutes later, the Indian lit a pinewood torch and led Harrer to a wooden chest. Inside was a collection of small cotton bags, each carefully sewn up, containing all that Harrer had left in the Indian's care the year before. The devotion and loyalty of the man was astounding. He laid before the hungry, footsore fugitive a meal which, after more than a week of living rough looked like a banquet. The Indian gave Harrer as much food as he could carry, a woollen blanket, woollen trousers and a shawl. And when Harrer left, two nights after he had arrived, the Indian insisted on walking part of the way with him.

Eventually, Harrer prevailed on the Indian to turn back and so, just after midnight, he set off alone again on the next leg of his journey, to the nomad village of Nelang. Harrer could not help feeling some trepidation as he approached the village. It was here, a year before, that an Indian policeman had put an end to his escape when he guessed that Harrer was not the Kashmiri pilgrim he pretended to be. This second time, though, Harrer had chosen his time well. He was a month earlier than in 1943, and there were no nomads in Nelang, no policemen and no officials.

However, to Harrer's surprise and delight, he did find, already camped in one of the houses, the other four fake 'Indians' who had walked out of Dehra Dun with him nearly a fortnight before. One of them, unfortunately, was in a bad state. Sattler, a German, was suffering from mountain sickness, an affliction that could only worsen when the time came to move on from Nelang. From there, it was up all the way, to heights that would top 5,000 metres. Poor Sattler was sure he would never survive the journey. There was nothing for him to do but to return to Dehra Dun and surrender. But he did promise the others – Harrer, two other Austrians, Peter Aufschneiter and Bruno Triepel, and Hans Kopp, a German from Berlin – that he would wait two days before giving himself up to allow them the best chance of getting across the border and into Tibet.

Harrer and his three companions regretfully parted company with Sattler. All the same, not long after they left Nelang to work their

Harrer's faith in the loyalty of his Indian friend is not misplaced

way towards the frontier, they knew Sattler had made the right decision. For soon, they were marching and climbing in regions where the going became more and more gruelling. Freezing, bone-chilling winds stormed through the valleys and along the passes, cutting through light khaki clothes that had been meant for the hot, sun-baked plains of Dehra Dun. As the four men struggled along, at times scaling heights that stood 5,500 metres above sea level, the air grew thinner and they found themselves gasping for breath. Every step became a monumental effort and the lack of oxygen made them all feel sick and giddy.

They were hungry, too. All that was left of their food a week after leaving Nelang was flour, which they mixed to a paste with water and cooked on hot stones into something roughly resembling a cake. But at last, on 17th May, 1944, less than three weeks after their escape from Dehra Dun, Harrer, Aufschneiter, Kopp and Triepel reached the top of the Tsang-Chokla pass. They were nearly 5,000 metres up. Nearby along the path there were welcome signs that the place was known to human beings. Small heaps of stones topped by prayer flags showed where devout Buddhist Tibetans had made offerings to their gods.

Beyond that stretched a seemingly endless vista of more high mountains and deep valleys. But however bleak and inhospitable it looked, it was the one sight all four men had longed to see. The Tsang-Chokla pass marked the border with India. Beyond that lay Tibet. Heinrich Harrer's third escape had proved to be third time lucky.

For Heinrich Harrer the snow-covered peaks and the green verdant valleys of the Himalayas not only mark the border between India and Tibet but between captivity and freedom

CHAPTER 16

Aftermath of Arnhem

*He pulled a trapdoor
out of the carpet of leaves and
loose earth, revealing a black hole beneath
with a rough wooden ladder
leading downwards.*

The carefully laid, carefully prepared plan had gone wrong. Colonel Graeme Warrack, ADMS (Chief Doctor) of the British First Airborne Division, realised that only too well as he lay cramped, aching and hungry inside his hideout in the roof of the hospital barracks at Appledoorn, Holland. The voices of the Germans talking in the room below that late October morning in 1944 were muffled by the ceiling. Warrack understood little of their language. But what he could comprehend was enough to tell him he was still in strongly held enemy territory, and that the British troops

he had hoped would rescue him were still some distance away.

'Englander – Nijmegen,' the Germans were saying. 'Deutsches – Arnhem – Wageningen – Amerongen – Utrecht.'

In map terms, that meant the British were 40 kilometres away across the River Rhine at Nijmegen. Straddling those 40 kilometres was a string of strong points, stretching from Arnhem to Utrecht, all of them still in German hands. As far as Warrack could gather, British forces were having a hard time making any progress. It could be weeks, even months, before they broke through to Apple-doorn. By that time, Warrack grimly reflected, he might well have died from starvation in his two-metre square bolthole. It was a distressing revelation. Bad enough, Warrack thought, to be involved once in a potentially successful venture gone wrong. To be involved twice was intolerable.

Graeme Warrack had first tasted this bitter pill after parachuting down at Arnhem with the First Airborne Division on 17th September, 1944. This strike behind the German lines was going to bring the Second World War to a speedy close – or so everyone believed. The Arnhem paratroops, together with others dropped simultaneously at

The paratroop drop at Arnhem was the beginning of a chain of disastrous events

Nijmegen and Eindhoven, would capture the bridges across the Dutch rivers Maas, Waal and Rhine. That done, Allied forces would sweep across into the plains of northern Germany, then on to the Ruhr and the German heartland. In theory, an unstoppable and triumphant advance. In the event, a disaster.

The air drops, codenamed Operation Market Garden, went seriously awry and nowhere more so than at Arnhem. Here, Warrack's division was trapped by unexpectedly fierce German resistance. Soon, they were ringed by artillery fire and mortar bombardment and with food and ammunition running low, were being forced to retreat. Although 2,200 paratroops managed to get out of the Arnhem area and reach British-held territory on the night of 26th September, large numbers were left behind dead, wounded or as prisoners.

It was the fate as well as the duty of army doctors like Graeme Warrack to remain with the wounded, and with them, he was captured by the Germans. Not that this put thoughts of escape out of his mind. Far from it. As Warrack worked in the hospital ward at Appledoorn barracks, getting as many wounded as possible fit enough for transport into Germany, he mulled over several plans for getting away.

Warrack was not, of course, the only one. Appledoorn teemed with plans for escape and prisoners, including the other doctors and the less badly wounded, were all preoccupied with this one purpose. British soldiers vanished into the bushes near the hospital and were not seen there again. Patients, once sufficiently recovered, jumped out of ward windows and hid in bales of straw, shrubberies or clumps of trees before slipping off by dark into the surrounding countryside. One of Warrack's fellow doctors made a daring getaway when he tracked his way by compass from Appledoorn to the Rhine: he waited for a suitably dark night, then swam the 200 metres across the river to rejoin the British forces on the other side.

Straightforward escapes like these were not, however, open to Graeme Warrack, for he was far more conspicuous than any of the other prisoners. First, he was senior medical officer at Appledoorn, and as such, a prisoner the Germans would quickly miss. Second, Warrack was very tall – 1·9 metres – and going slightly bald: he would be very easy for the Germans to spot and recapture.

Eventually, though, Warrack found the solution, or so he thought; he discovered a space in the roof of his office in which he could hide. He stocked it with food, water, blankets, clothes, a shaving kit and other necessities. Then, when the last British wounded had left Appledoorn, around the middle of October, he climbed up through the trapdoor, closed it after himself and settled down for what he fancied would be a relatively short stay. Somewhere to the south, he could already hear the distant boom of guns. It could only be a few days before British forces would arrive and he could emerge into liberty.

But the 'few days' stretched to a fortnight, with the British forces no nearer Appledoorn and Warrack virtually marooned. Before long, he lost count of the hour after cramped, painful hour he spent immobile so that the German officer in the room below would not realise there was a fugitive directly above his head. Water was getting short. Food was running out. At any time, his foot might accidentally scrape on the rafters, he might drop something or he might sneeze, cough or make other similar mistakes that would give his presence away.

When the room below was empty, Warrack risked coming down from the roof space to stretch his aching legs. But he could not count on his luck lasting out indefinitely and it was likely that he would soon find himself surprised and caught by some casual visitor. It could not go on, particularly not after the snatched conversation Warrack overheard early on 28th October in the room below his hiding place. The information the Germans unwittingly gave him then made it absolutely certain, instead of just possible, that his personal plan to elude them had gone the same dismal way as the whole Arnhem air drop. There was only one thing left to do. Somehow, he had to break out, dodge the German soldiers billetted at Appledoorn barracks, get through the surrounding wire and the German troops deployed in the area, and cross the Rhine to reach the British lines.

The night this enterprise began – the night of 29th October – was brilliantly moonlit, frosty and still. At 11 pm Warrack quietly let himself down through the trapdoor into the vacant room below, taking with him his few belongings and the remainder of his food. He crept to the window. A quick glance outside seemed to assure him that the place was deserted, but just as he was pushing the window open to clamber out, he saw a guard. The man was only one metre away.

Warrack after a fortnight in hiding, is nearly spotted as he tries to get away

Warrack dropped back, crawled under the table and listened. Footsteps moved past the window. The guard's rifle gave a click as he pulled it up on his shoulder. Then, to Warrack's intense relief, he heard the guard walking off. When he moved back to the window, Warrack could see the man about 20 metres away, with his back to him.

Warrack looked up into the sky. In less than five minutes, the moon would illuminate the window like a searchlight. The first pale beams were just creeping round when Warrack put a leg over the sill, touched ground, pulled the other leg after him and ran over the slippery wet cobbles outside to a patch of

The Dutch people did everything in their power to assist the escape of Allied troops

shadow between two buildings. He paused. The next shadow lay about 30 metres away, by a stable. As Warrack ran up and pressed himself back against the wall, a horse inside the stable stamped and shook its halter. Warrack held his breath. Seconds passed, but no-one came to investigate. Warrack crept on towards a fence backed by thick undergrowth. He dropped to his hands and knees and crawled along the fence until he reached a gap. Only 40 metres away, a German sentry was pacing up and down. Wincing with trepidation at every slight noise he made, Warrack wriggled through the gap into the field on the other side, then on past some factory buildings and a house to reach the road. At any moment, Warrack expected to hear the dreaded shout 'Alt! Alt!' and the pounding of German feet pursuing him, but nothing happened. All was quiet. So far, he thought, so good.

He set off across the moonlit fields, making for the railway line which his map told him led to Ede, about 18 kilometres to the south. There, he knew a group of British paratroops were hiding out, waiting for the chance to cross the Rhine. Warrack walked steadily through the night, pausing only to suck a few frosted oak leaves to quench his thirst and once, to dodge behind a tree when he heard footsteps coming close. When daylight came, he hid himself in a clump of trees and waited for the hours to pass until it was dark again.

His muscles, stiffened by lack of exercise, were cramped and aching, and he was glad of the day's rest, even though it rained for two hours, leaving him drenched, cold and shivering. As soon as it grew dark enough, he set off again. He was following a fence close to some bushes when, suddenly, he saw a cottage about 30 metres away. There were lights inside and faintly, the sound of girls chattering and laughing reached Warrack's ears.

Common sense warned him not to go any closer. There might be Germans billetted in the cottage, and even if there were not, contacting any Dutch people could put them in danger. But common sense lost. Warrack found himself creeping up to the cottage window, where he saw two pretty, young Dutch girls in the kitchen. Twice he tapped on the pane the morse code for 'V', the 'Victory' signal well known all over occupied Europe. Seconds later, one of the girls opened the door.

If Tineke Reint was momentarily startled when she saw Graeme Warrack standing outside, it was hardly surprising. He looked a total tramp: dirty and thoroughly unkempt with two weeks' beard on his chin, muffled in a blanket with a loaf of bread sticking out of his jacket pocket and his grimy red paratrooper's beret pulled down over his eyes. However, as Warrack soon discovered, he could not have come across a better place, nor a better family to ask for food, shelter and help. He had arrived by pure chance at what was known in the furtive world of escape as a 'good' house. The Reints, whose cottage was near the village of Otterlo, had contacts with the Dutch Underground and had already hidden several fugitives, including a British officer and a family of Jews. What was more, they were well equipped for this clandestine rescue work. Some distance away from their cottage, in the nearby woods, was their 'spare room' – an underground dugout about ten metres square and two metres high, lined with logs and straw and equipped with a ventilation shaft, a bucket and tins of food.

After he had eaten a simple, but very welcome meal, Graeme Warrack followed old man Reint out into the forest to where a small mound marked the entrance to the dugout. Reint pulled a trapdoor out of the carpet of leaves and loose earth, revealing a black hole beneath with a rough wooden ladder leading downwards. Warrack climbed down into the underground room. Reint stayed long enough to check that no glints of light from Warrack's candle were visible through the trapdoor and then set off back to his cottage.

Warm, dry, well fed and feeling safer than he had done for weeks, Warrack slept soundly through the night. Next morning, he enjoyed what had recently been an impossible luxury: he shaved. Before long, Tineke Reint arrived with his breakfast.

The days that followed quickly took on a routine – meals, chats with Tineke and her sister Hanneke, and a few hours playing solo card games. Sometimes Warrack could hear people walking through the woods, sometimes the noise of cars moving along the road

nearby. At first, he found it all quite pleasant, even relaxing, but as the days went by, the thought constantly nagged him that the Reint family were running enormous and terrible risks in sheltering him. Every time Tineke, Hanneke or any of the Reint family came out to give him food, bring him a quilt or a hot water bottle or had any contact with him, they might be caught by Germans combing the woods. It would not take much imagination for them to guess what the family was doing and the punishments would be swift and savage: instant death for the men of the family, the women hauled off to concentration camps and the cottage burned to the ground. It had

Rows of marble slabs today commemorate the hundreds of soldiers who lost their lives in Operation Market Garden

happened to other Dutch families. It could happen to the Reints.

These fears of the tragedy he might be bringing upon his hosts lent added spice to Warrack's feelings of relief when after ten days, Piet von Arnhem, of the Dutch Underground, arrived to tell him that he would be moving quite soon. Guides would come, with bicycles, and ride with him to a spot north of Ede where other escapers were to meet. There, battledress and sten guns would be issued and food distributed, and more guides would lead the escapers to the river where boats would be waiting to row them across.

It was an impudent plan but, von Arnhem assured Warrack, it was feasible. British patrols had been making nightly forays across the Rhine into German-held territory for some time now, and the Germans could easily mistake a large body of escapers for one of these intruding groups. Only three weeks before, during October, 150 men had been helped across the Rhine in precisely this way. Von Arnhem left Warrack hopeful. If a plan could work once, Warrack reasoned, it could work again.

*The escape plan having failed, Warrack is surrounded
by attacking German soldiers*

Ten nights later, Graeme Warrack was lying
face down in a ditch in woodland about one
kilometre from the river with German bullets
whistling overhead and thudding into the
wet earth all around him. The escape plan
that had worked once had failed as far as he
and his fellow escapers were concerned. The
woods were full of shouts and the screams of
wounded men. Rifles cracked. Sten guns and
machine guns rattled and grenades exploded,
sending vibrations shuddering through the
earth. Flares were being fired into the air to
illuminate the scene. The Germans, present in
great numbers, had ambushed them.

154

Everything had gone according to plan until they had come to a narrow path in the woods. The departure from the Reints' cottage, the bicycle journey to the rendezvous near Ede, the would-be escapers (109 of them apart from Warrack) moving in four groups towards the river – all had been accomplished smoothly. Then, suddenly, just as Warrack's group was moving in single file through the trees, a German shouted 'Alt!' nearby. The escapers scattered, weaving through the trees in an attempt to elude the German patrol they had so unexpectedly encountered. Only seven men got across the Rhine that night. One or two were killed, several wounded. Most were captured and a handful, including Graeme Warrack, managed to get away.

Disappointed, dispirited and soaked by rain as they went, Warrack, together with an American pilot, John Low and a Dutch civilian called Ronald, trekked back towards Otterlo. By 20th November, the three of them were huddled into the Reints' 'spare room' beneath the forest floor.

There, Warrack remained for the next four weeks, waiting impatiently for the chance to try again. In the end it took several tries before at long last he succeeded. All sorts of difficulties frustrated him and the other escapers: the river currents were too strong; the crosswinds were too dangerous; there was a heavy, two-day snowfall; the moon was too bright; or the British Army group with whom the Dutch Underground was in constant contact warned them that the Germans patrolling the river banks were too alert.

Then, in the first week of February 1945, more than three months after he had slipped out of the hospital at Appledoorn, Graeme Warrack stepped into a perilously rocking canoe moored in a canal and with two Dutchmen, Lippy and Jan, in two other canoes, began to paddle the choppy, wind-whipped 20 kilometres along waterways and two Rhine tributaries to freedom.

Physically, this was the most gruelling part of Warrack's long escape. With his two companions he paddled through the turbulent waters, hauled his canoe over locks, baled out water, and once had to lie for two uncomfortable hours in a clump of bushes with a storm howling around them, sending down great curtains of rain sharp as whiplashes. All the way, the three men had to be on the alert for Germans. There were machine gun nests close to the waterway, searchlight batteries were nearby and there was a wireless station manned by Germans whose mast was clearly silhouetted against the night sky as the canoes drifted past.

The last obstacle was the most perilous of all: a ferry crossing point on the River Waal, only about 200 metres wide and guarded on either side by blockhouses with machine guns.

By this time, only one of the canoes was still afloat. Warrack climbed in with Jan, leaving Lippy behind to be picked up later. Then, they cast off, forcing their canoe through waves so strong that they cracked like pistol shots against the sides of the boat.

Warrack could feel the soreness of blisters on his hands as he paddled steadily past the blockhouses, and by the time the canoe had slipped past the ferry point, the paddle handle was sticky with blood from his lacerated hands. A creek opened up on one side of the river bank. Warrack and Jan turned the boat up it and were moving past the flat, silent terrain when a figure suddenly loomed up out of the darkness. A rifle clicked and a voice called: 'Halt! Who goes there?'

Warrack felt an overwhelming relief. The voice, the words it spoke, and control of the territory on which its owner stood were all English.

The final part of the journey was physically the most gruelling, and hovered on the brink of disaster